DEFINING MOMENTS

Stories of Magic when Determination Intersects Destiny

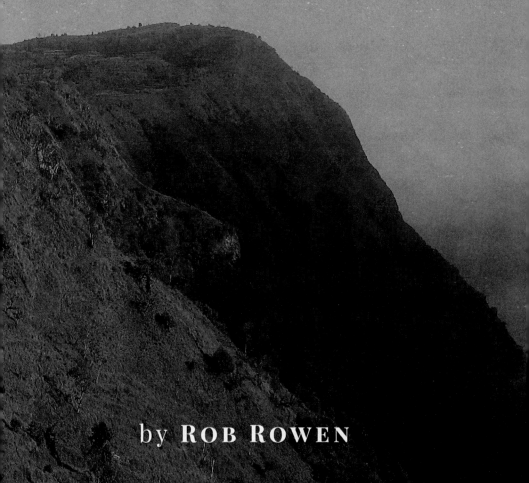

by ROB ROWEN

Edited by
Dawn Medlock and Kimberly Kudar

Cover Design by
Greg Cordell

Graphic Editing by
Camilo Nieto, Havana, Cuba

Some of the Photos by
Rob Rowen

Printed by
Hardwick Printers

Copyright 2021 by
Rob Rowen

ISBN
978-1-63795-501-7

*Dedicated to all who seek
to heal the world.*

Contents

Preface

How do you thank those who made you who you are and this book possible? First, my parents, Jack and Lucille Rowen, who instilled in you that community mattered, check! They have traveled on, but their legacy lives on. Next profound thanks to my wife, my muse, Suzanne Golden, who married me ten plus years ago and indeed my mate. She supported all my crazy traveling worldwide and time spent healing the world in my small way. Perhaps she was behind me because she, too, is a hopeless (in a good way) healer. She is dedicated to understanding dog's health, becoming a practitioner of massage and other healing techniques, and fostering the most abused fur babies; she understands that we have to act deep in her heart. Of course, I have to thank the other participants in this book who have enthralled me in their stories and inspired me to get out of bed on a cool Florida morning at 5:00 am to start writing this. They wrote this book by being such luminaries, showing what is possible and making this world a better place to live in. Also, one of those stories includes my daughter, who continues to inspire me in her ability to juggle so much so well and is one of my life's advisors. In the nuts of bolts of writing this book, I had help from my tennis buddy, Keith Medlock's wife Dawn, who helped edit it, and my newer friend Greg Cordell instantly knew what the book cover should look like and showed his exceptional creative talent to me. I also want to shout out to my many international friends who have taught me so much and changed my worldview. Now it is time for you to delve into a world you will find worth visiting. Rob

Prologue

A small village in Tennessee finally got electricity. This was a big deal, and everyone soon had their house wired and hooked in. One day the meter reader dropped by one of his customers. He said to her, "you have had electricity now for many months, and something must be wrong," He then mentioned that he has not seen the meter dial move in all that time. He figured something must be broken. "No, she said it works just fine. Every day I turn on my lights, light my candles, and then shut the electricity off. For some, you can have power hooked up but never figure out how to use it, and for those others, it changes their lives. In this book, you will read of people who had the power turned on, and you can feel the electrical charge that their use has made of it.

Author's Note

Inspirational moments that have reshaped lives

The idea for this book was a long time coming. In my life, I had various and unusual opportunities to meet people with stories to tell that left an indelible mark upon my soul. In the last few years, we have lost so many heroes. Or who we thought were our heroes. Bill Cosby, a sweet TV father, turns out to drug women, allegations against Charlie Rose, Dustin Hoffman, and Al Franken were particularly painful for me. Others probably felt the same about Bill O'Reilly and Mario Cuomo. We are all human, and all of us can be seduced by power, money, and fame, so I submit to you a new group of heroes. These are your everyday heroes. They are you and me, faced with challenges that seem insurmountable. Some are people who every day pass by the tragedies of life, and instead of muttering "Somebody should do something about that," stop and become that somebody who puts aside their life's course to make that difference. Others are people that life took a left turn when they planned to go straight, and it is how they choose to deal with it that will inspire you.

Travel with me across the globe and across the spectrum of life to meet these people, and let's honor our true heroes together.

photo: *Thomas Wilkins.*

chapter 1

THOMAS WILKINS,

The Boy From The Ghetto
Makes Musical Magic

Thomas is one of the keys to why I wrote this book. While Chairing the Speaker Committee for the South Tampa Chamber, I came across this man's story many years ago. I was always looking to bring different speakers from the norm, hoping to inspire our Chamber. Like most business organizations, our Chamber likes to expose the members to new ways to do business and be successful. I thought that was great, but I tried to bring different experiences for the members. So I choose people I thought might not teach them how to sell more or market better, but inspiration spurs their creative juices. I think this was about twenty-seven years ago when I met Thomas, and his story so resonated with me that I found myself sharing his story from time to time.

I was at a party in the neighborhood I used to live in St. Petersburg. My wife and I were back there, closing up our rental house and loading our final furnishings in a pod as the last part of our move to Greenville, SC. I decided to walk over to this holiday party to say goodbye to our neighbors. Everyone had on name tags, and I find myself standing next to a tall, elegant black man named Tom. I look up and ask, Thomas Wilkins? And he said yes. I proceeded to tell him that I had just told his story recently, and lo and behold, there he is. Early the next morning, and I mean early morning, around 5 am, Suzanne, my wife, who was suffering from that dreaded winter cold, was in the living room of our rental house coughing. Most of our furniture was in Greenville's new home; she was our couch in the living room, hoping not to disturb me. Alas, I lay in bed, and my mind wandered to the serendipity of meeting Thomas Wilkins after all these years. Then I started thinking about other amazing human beings whose stories I knew. I realized they, too, needed to be told, and I was off to the races. At 5 am, the house was silent. I went into what remained of our office in the house, a desk and a chair and my laptop. I was inspired and full of ideas and started writing this book. I am excited to start you off with the inspirational story of Thomas Wilkins. Enjoy!

Thomas grew up in Norfolk, Virginia, blessed with one of the most hardworking mothers you could have. She struggled in raising her son, trying to stay off welfare. Being black and a single mother in the south was tough. She worked as a nurse's aide in several nursing homes. I hope you remember this was in the middle of the Civil Rights movement, and even in this Navy town, there were plenty of issues. She taught Thomas the basics, respect of school, church, and his elders, and that he had to do his homework whether she was around. Often she was out working to pay for their rent and food. He says the most important lesson he learned was to be accountable and make responsible choices. His neighbors picked up the slack. For a boy being alone, this could be a prescription for disaster. His musical interests began when he was given his first little whistle in music class. He loved making sounds and tried to figure out how to make songs he heard on TV. His transformational moment came in 3rd grade when his school went on a class trip. It was to a building he could see from his window in the projects, a building he had no idea what it was for; it could have been a jail for all he knew. When Thomas walked into this building, he discovered a Conductor with his symphony. The power of music was overwhelming to him. He says, "I was toast, totally hooked." The first thing that happened was this large group of musicians tuning up their instruments. The Conductor was not out yet. When he came out, he had an aura around him. The Conductor was Maestro Russell Stanger, and he pointed to the snare drummer, and they played Star-Spangled Banner. What blew him away was the man with the baton in his hand who seemed to be making the music happen. He watched the orchestra, but his attention was on the conductor with all his passion.

That night when his mother came home from work, he told her he wanted to be a Conductor. That began a long road starting with 4th grade learning to play the violin, then in 5th grade the cello. Finally, in Junior High School, he taught himself the trumpet fingering to be in the band. In most schools, particularly his inner-city school, the music program was underfunded, and you had to buy your instruments. His mother never had that kind of money, so when the band director told him he could take the tuba home, that became his instrument of choice. His teachers in school gave him lessons since he never had a formal private lesson. He never had a tutor until he was in college and devoted himself to studying music full time.

He told me most people who study music don't become musicians; only the freaks are the ones who get through it. In, school the purpose of music education is to create music appreciation, not musicians.

Thomas makes an incisive point: he says, "once the moment I fell in love with music, all my life choices were made for me by default." I realized I had to hang around with like-minded people if I was to succeed. Thomas began the road to his music dreams, and he had many questions. He wondered, do I dream of going to college? Wilkins decided to apply himself, and even when there was no adult supervision, no family member around, instead of losing himself in something mindless, practiced. Thomas remembers when he could finally go to the library by himself, he would get an album and listen to it with earphones while he was there. These are things most children don't have to work to do.

His drive enabled him to go to the Shenandoah Conservatory of Music. This decision required him to get some loans to augment the small scholarship he earned. He picked that school because he could be a Brass Choir student conductor in his freshman year. He later got a graduate degree from the prestigious New England Conservatory in Boston. He started conducting at the undergraduate level and obtained his Masters's in Conducting. In 1982 he landed his first job teaching at North Park College in Chicago and later at the University of Tennessee in Chattanooga. However, he wanted to conduct in Richmond, and he applied and got it the second time around, coming home.

Here he was years later sitting down with that Maestro, the conductor that had been his inspiration to him. He remembers the joy of finally meeting this man. He had appeared on that podium like a god so large, so powerful. It was one of those amazing moments for him, the completion of a complicated circle. Life is full of circles and thinking of all the hard choices Thomas had made to be there. I can only imagine what he was thinking when he picked up the baton to begin working with the musicians. The boy who walked into the Symphony Hall to the man conducting that same orchestra required so much. So much desire, so much perseverance, so much love. Do we have that kind of desire? Remember being from a family without money,

so poor he couldn't even take home an instrument for most of his childhood. His ability to listen to music required a trip to the library. My admiration for his drive is profound. So let's return to his story and how he and I intersected.

When I met him, he was the Resident Conductor for the Florida Orchestra under Maestro Jacha Ling. In Tampa Bay, this was where a large part of musical growth happened. He had more conducting responsibility, though he was still taking lessons. He got to follow his dream, which was to work with children and help be the catalyst for them to fall in love with music. One of his most satisfying jobs was being the conductor for Young Person's Concerts with the prestigious Boston Symphony.

He realized now the amount of opportunity to make bad choices are profound. If you awaken something in a young person no matter their surroundings, no matter their lack of money, they will find a way to achieve their goals. Maybe they will have a leg up on those with all the money and supportive family because it is a fact they have to do it the hard way that drives them to their very success. As he advocated for more educational opportunities in the inner city, a man said that schools are costly and not worth funding; Wilkins replied that poverty was much more expensive. Thomas has since spent a lot of his time working with youth to be that spark plug. He made a choice that will keep on inspiring other youngsters to follow their passions, and for that, he was an easy first chapter.

I asked him what music he would take if he was on a deserted island in our interview. I found it a fascinating list and wanted to share it with you. Mahler Symphony 1, Naima by the incomparable John Coltrane, One of Miles Davis's greatest hits Green Dolphin Street. Then he moves to James Taylor's Keep My Heart Out of Sight, the music of Earth Wind and Fire, and finally one of the all-time great songs and a favorite of mine, Louis Armstrong's What a Wonderful World. And it is people like Thomas Wilkins who make this planet a wonderful world.

I asked him how we could help bring children in the inner city to grow as he did. He said, "I am closely associated with the YOLA (Youth Orchestra Los Angeles) program at the L.A. Philharmonic. Inspired by the El Sistema program from Venezuela that Gustavo Dudamel has made famous. It has been very successful in giving opportunities to children. Programs like it have sprung up all over the country, and they are all connected.

photo: *Jessi, Elio and the boys*

chapter 2

JESSI AND ELIO NAVARRO,
(My daughter and son in law)

Sometimes The Inspirations
Come From Those Close To You

You can see how Thomas Wilkins was such a catalyst for this book. The following story will explore another defining moment of my life as we learn about what happened when my daughter decided to become a counselor at Muscular Dystrophy Camp and began a chain of events that will be part of several subsequent stories.

My son-in-law, Elio Navarro, is one of these people with a story to tell. Elio was diagnosed at two and a half years with a severe disease. His first eight years were just a regular boy with a normal boy who dreams of living a life like everyone else. His obstacle, his mountain, came in the form of Spinal Muscular Atrophy, a severe form of Muscular Dystrophy. Early on, his father placed him in front of a computer and encouraged him to learn computer skills, and he became adept at it. He lost much of his mobility throughout his childhood and schooling and learned to operate a motorized wheelchair. During that time, he gained and channeled his time, becoming a whiz at computers. Elio was a great student. His intelligence and drive carried him through the University of South Florida to get his bachelor's degree in Information Systems and his MBA before age twenty-three. He also excelled as an intern at Verizon and was named the National Intern of the Year before hiring him full-time. He has developed software programs for companies across healthcare, finance, and marketing throughout his career, improving their efficiencies and profitability. His following field was developing apps for all types of industries. When NCAA Basketball Finals came to Tampa, information came through an app he had created.

Elio was also a pioneer for many in the disability community when he purchased a wheelchair van and learned to drive it. He was a proficient driver, and he traveled all over Tampa Bay in it. He showed the van to many other kids with Muscular Dystrophy and encouraged them to expand their dreams. He aimed to inspire them to drive and pursue exciting careers without being held back by their physical limitations.

Elio and his father were huge sports fans. One day he read a story about a man named Jerry Frick in New Mobility Magazine. Jerry's article highlighted a sport you could play while seated in a power wheelchair. Elio quickly called him up and was enthralled. It was Power Soccer, and this was becoming a major sport in the disabled world, and it required two things. The first was the ability to move your chair in reaction to the ball and your teammates. The second was using your intelligence in understanding team dynamics and strategy. Elio created the first Power Soccer team in the Tampa Bay area, and it was so successful. When more players were interested, he ended up creating a second team. His vision for giving young men and women in power chairs an outlet to compete was warmly received in an up-and-coming international sport. It was fascinating to see young people in chairs being outfitted with chair guards and learn how to pass and hit a large soccer ball. For many, learning how to control their chair and learn team skills would help them succeed in other parts of their lives. Elio trained intensely and quickly became one of the top players in the US. His outstanding play and court sense elevated him to the USA team heading to their first Power Soccer International Tournament in Japan.

The USA fought its way to the Gold Match and was victorious. This excitement and success of Team USA brought

photo: *Elio playing Power Soccer.*

even more passion and interest back to the US Power Soccer community. It was during that tournament, Elio realized that no US networks were covering or broadcasting these games or rarely any disability sports. I remember when I was young, there was a show, The Wide World of Sports. One time they covered some of Rugby's sport, often called 'Murder Ball,' because of the intensity and physicality of the game. The Paralympics was the showcase to the public, but only if they broadcast it. Elio decided to record the games, so others in the US would have a chance to see them.

He set up his father with a video camera to record the games. It was a fantastic experience for those who watched people with similar disabilities being athletes and competing at the highest level. The filming grew into the idea to cover all wheelchair and disability sports as they, too, deserved exposure. The recording of these games was a first for the Disability community. It was a fantastic experience for those that got to watch people with similar disabilities being athletes and competing at the highest level.

So my daughter Jessi and Elio created a website called X-Able.com as a vehicle for education and celebrated this community's invisible athletes. In New Jersey, the World Disability Expo was one of the first events they decided to cover. I was excited when they asked me to join the team and be the broadcaster at the Power Soccer games they organized at the Expo. Plus, I got to do some interviewing of exhibitors and different products and services they offered. I enjoyed the challenge as I was a huge sports fan, although I did not have much experience with disability sports. I will have to continue this part of the story later, as we are talking about Elio and my daughter.

Now you are getting a taste of how Elio rolled, a little pun here, he would use his computers and business expertise to engage others to make a difference. They also created a company, Power Soccer Shop, which made products for that sport easily usable and affordable. Elio changed my life, but I didn't see it coming. It was many years earlier that Elio came into our family. It started when my daughter went to Muscular Dystrophy Camp as a counselor. Her birthday that year included several friends from MDA camp. When those three chairs rolled into our house and our lives, it was a huge milestone in our lives. My being brought into this community was the beginning of changing my understanding of this community's needs and heroes, as you will see in other stories. Honestly, my first reaction to Jessi choosing someone who spent much of his life in a chair was dismay. I wondered if she understood what she was giving up for love. It shows great determination and love to see somebody so completely. However, what she gained was so much more, and it did not take long to get past the limitations Elio faced to see his greatness. We got to see Jessi and Elio's story broadcast on national television on the Jerry Lewis Telethon supporting Muscular Dystrophy. Like many of you, I watched the Telethon every year as Jerry entertained and welcomed the best talents of the world to join him on this worthy cause. Little did I ever expect to see my daughter on that stage with the love of her life. They traveled to California to be interviewed by Jan Karl, highlighting how a couple, one able-bodied and one disabled, have joined their lives together. It was a special moment for all of us. I now have two amazing grandsons who will grow up in this loving household where nothing is unachievable.

chapter 3

AZIM KHAMISA

*Sometimes In Tragedy
Is the Great Spark Of Clarity*

You can tell how personal this story is for me, but let me take you far away to distant Uganda and share a story of another father making a tough choice that led to even tougher choices.

Sometimes what you are looking for comes to you without much effort. This next story is what that is all about. It is the story of a father of Ismail heritage living and running a business in Uganda. His name is Azim Khamisa, and he and his family were living In Kenya, having fled from Uganda during the brutal regime of dictator Idi Amin. Azim realizes he wants his children to grow up safely, and that place is not Uganda. So he picks the United States, and that is where his transformation begins. Fast forward approximately ten years, and his son, Tariq, is living in San Diego. He is going to college and making ends meet, working weekends delivering pizza. It was a Saturday night when he delivers a pizza order to a building. It turns out

the address is a setup, but he does not know that yet, so he goes back to his car with the pizza. There he is met by a gang of young boys waiting to get the pizza from him. He ignores them, refusing to give up the pizza, putting it back into his trunk, and getting into the car. As he starts to back up, a fourteen-year-old boy comes to his window, raises his hand holding a gun, and fires. The doctor later called it the perfect shot. Perfect in that the trajectory of the bullet destroyed three major organs. Tariq died drowning in his own blood. I cannot imagine the grief and anger that Azim went through. How could this happen in America? How could this happen to his son? How could this happen to him and his wife? There is no way to describe the depths of his despair and how close he came to suicide. Our children are not supposed to die before us. The fourteen-year-old boy who shot him, Tony, was sentenced to prison for 24 years. This justice did little to dispel any of his pain. Now the story becomes inspiring. Azim goes through a hellish nine months of depression and soul searching, having difficulty dealing with his son's loss to senseless violence. One thought that kept coming up was what could have caused a 14-year old child to kill him for a pizza. He was shocked that we have a society where children kill children. As a US citizen, even though a victim, he felt he had to take his share of responsibility for how this could happen and decided to dedicate his life to youth violence challenges. He was wondering who was the enemy here? Was the enemy the fourteen-year-old who fell through our society's cracks handed a gun, not realizing what it meant? Who among us was prepared at fourteen to understand life and death decisions and act correctly under pressure from your peers, his street family? This tragedy was how Azim was inspired to start his Foundation to do something real about this tragedy. He decided on three mandates. The first mandate was to save children's lives, the second to empower them with the right choices, and the third to teach the principles of non-violence.

In his search for understanding and healing, he had come upon the Bardo, a Tibetan Buddhist concept. The teaching says, 'Compassionate acts undertaken in the name of the departed are the spiritual currency that speeds the soul's journey.' This simple directive struck Akim. I met Azim Khamisa at a Rotary Peace and Conflict Conference in Greenville, South Carolina. Listening to this man talking about empathy and forgiveness was captivating. He took this work to another level when he asked the young man's grandfather, who killed his son, to join him in this crusade. Tony's grandfather, Ples Felix, had served in Vietnam in the Green Berets. Ples was shocked and horrified that his grandson had pulled that trigger, killed another child, and was instantly on board. This fantastic story of two men who had lost their children, one to death and one to prison, working together, is about redemption and forgiveness. He was thankful for this opportunity, a Muslim and a Christian dedicated to this work. To this day, they have given over 1000 presentations together, specializing in children in sixth through ninth grades.

In sixth grade, his grandson Tony joined the gang and was in eighth when he fired the bullet that would end Tariq's life. Ples Felix had tried to be involved with his grandson's life, but it is easy for a child to be influenced by the wrong people.

One of the first things they do at one of their school events is to ask the students who have had someone they know die from violence. Azim holds these classes in inner-city schools, and so the response is usually most of the children. The next question is, how many would like to get revenge? Again almost all of those children raised their hands. It is how easily violence grows, and that is why two people on both sides of the same horrible act have such creditability in teaching that there is a different way to act.

Now I get to tell you a story inside a story. Azim says that after one of the school training's on non-violence, the class discussed one of the messages they had been the topic of that training. The subject of the saying "You don't know me until you walked a mile in my shoes" was the subject, and when the teacher asked if anyone had a story to tell one boy, Alejandro kept raising his hand. The teacher did not want to call him as he had been the problem kid in the class, and she did want to ruin the lesson, but finally, she did call him. Alejandro told this story. He was walking in another neighborhood when a black kid started giving him dirty looks. His first thought was he could beat him up, but then he decided to walk over and confront him about why he was looking at him that way. The other kid said his brother had been shot by a black kid right in this spot the other day. Alejandro looked at him and said, I know what you mean; my favorite uncle died here six months ago. He then reached out and put his hand on the other kid's shoulder, and they both were sharing the same thoughts and realizations. This example is how we can change the world; this is how we can make a difference.

The famous 13th-century Persian poet Rumi said in a poem, "Be a lamp or a lifeboat, or a ladder. Help someone's soul to heal. Walk out of your house like a shepherd".

There are very few human beings like Azim Khamisa, and the work he does is so precious. If this story touches your soul, you can help children like Tony avoid the treacherous paths to violence by supporting the Tariq Khamisa Foundation, https// tkf.org/home-r/. You also can read more about his work in his four books.

photo: *Felix Ples, Tony and Azim*

photo: *Rob and JC Russo covering Wheelchair Soccer Nationals*

chapter 4

MY BECOMING A SPORTS BROADCASTER, MOVE OVER MARV ALBERT,

From Azim's story of grief turning into love which still gives me the shivers, let us return to my story and how I became an 'able-bodied man of the disability community. As you will remember from Elio's story, my son-in-law Elio and daughter Jessi asked me to announce a Power Soccer tournament in New Jersey as part of the Disabilities' Expo. I always loved sports and was a crazed NY Knicks fan and remember listening to Marv Albert calling the games in the days when that was the only way to follow your team. He had this knack for making it exciting, and when I was shooting baskets by myself, I would pretend to be announcing the game as the clock wound down, and my hero Walt Frazier, the star guard, would take the last shot at the buzzer. I loved the game of basketball, but alas, I was never very good at it, and my dreams of becoming an NBA star were never based in reality. So I was surprised to get the chance to be an announcer, the next best thing. So when asked by Elio and Jessi if I would help them out by announcing a tournament at this Disability Expo, I jumped at the chance. I was determined to do it right, and the first thing I did was do some research about the game, the players, the coaches, and the strategies. I guess I did a good enough job that I got the call to head across the state of Florida within a few weeks to cover a Quad Rugby tournament. The players' excitement and interest from the various businesses we met at the Expo gave Elio the idea to use a Foundation he had created to broadcast disability sports to the world via the website. So this became my vehicle for becoming the Voice of X-Able Sports. So off we went to Fort Lauderdale to cover the Knock and Roll Tournament. Remember, I was a novice to this and had never seen Quad Rugby played. My only exposure was by watching an excellent movie about this sport called Murder

photo: *With my color commentators*

Ball. The movie followed the battle between Team USA and Team Canada, coached by the former USA coach. The film brought out the intensity between the teams, making for both an educational and exciting movie. The chairs often collided while the players moved the ball across the court and over the goal line. During the games, there were many crashes, and chairs were over on their sides. It dispelled your belief of the players being fragile. You cannot find a more exciting game, and the teams playing were from all over the world. I believe there were teams from New Zealand, Canada, and Germany participating. Later that year, we covered the Quad Rugby National Championships. When I broadcasted a game, I would ask different people to be my color commentators. Sometimes it was a coach or a player, and one time I had two refs. I also enjoyed having some of the people featured in the Murder Ball movie sitting next to me and offering their insights. My favorite commentator was John Rosser, who played goalie for the Tidewater Piranhas in Division Two. Since he did not use his hands or arms, he used his shoulder to maneuver the Chair. When he wanted a drink, he used his mouth to get a straw from his shirt pocket. For me, the learning curve of being part of this community was never to underestimate what someone could do. He had the best sense of humor, and we always had the best time together.

I was covering a tournament. I forgot which one (I believe I did over 150 broadcasts in my short time as a sportscaster), and my preparation for these was to contact the teams and learn about the players and coaches looking for great stories to add color to the reporting we were doing. One day I got a call from Jessi, my daughter, and she told me she had gotten a case of popcorn sent to X-Able's address with my name on it. I remembered mentioning a team coach in a manual wheelchair who was also the popcorn company manager. I thought that would be interesting, showing that being disabled did not mean you could not succeed in business. I remember it was Pop Warner Pop Corn, so I ended my thought with, I hope it is good popcorn. I guess he wanted me to find out personally, and we had a lot of great popcorn after that.

One of my favorites was the Veteran's games in Omaha. Each year the Paralyzed Veteran of America, working with the Veteran Affairs Administration, put on the games. All disabled veterans are invited and compete in track and field, swimming, agility courses, and many sports. Jessi and I recruited many coaches from the disabled community to cover the many different games happening consecutively. One of her jobs was to upload the events of each day. She worked tirelessly, and we usually ate dinner after working around 8 pm and then went to bed to do it all over again. Even though it was about the competition, the loving support and sharing were outstanding.

From there, just about every two to three weeks, we were on the road covering sports. We covered many sports and logged over 150 broadcasts. It was one of the most exciting times in my life. You can watch some great games I covered by going to You Tube channel and pasting the X-Able disability media network in the search engine.

We traveled to Fort Lauderdale, Birmingham, Tulsa, Atlanta, Omaha, Chicago, and back to Omaha and then Minneapolis. I remember one young man coming up to me at the Nationals Championships for Power Soccer. He said he enjoyed my broadcasts. I said the power soccer ones? His response was no all of them. He had become a fan of watching Wheelchair Softball, Basketball, and the many others we covered. I then realized that the hunger for heroes in this community was something we were addressing and essential.

I felt that we had become quite the team. At first, Elio, Jessi, Gunnison, a close friend of theirs, and myself. Unfortunately, Elio ended up working, so mainly the three of us or just Jessi, my daughter, and me. I welcome you to watch some of these on the You Tube channel.

As I was finishing up the book I noticed that two of the athletes I mentioned in the book, Matt Scott and Steve Serio are competing in the 2021 Paralympics as part of the US team in Wheelchair Basketball. This is Matt's 5th time and Steve's 4th. I wish them well and hope they bring another gold medal home.

Your next story is about Juan Ortiz, one of the heroes of this book I met while covering a Wheelchair Softball tournament in Chicago.

photo: *X-Able team, Elio, Jessi, Gunther and me*

photo: *Juan and wife Maureen*

chapter 5

JUAN ORTIZ

A Story Of How You Can
Turn Water Into Wine

Juan was an only child growing up in the Southside of Chicago. With his father and mother divorced, his mother worked two jobs to keep them above water. This beginning is similar to Thomas Wilkin's story but shows the other path many of our children go down. Juan's mother was gone much of the time working, which left Juan plenty of time hanging with the wrong crowd. He is not proud of the trouble he got into at that time, but it was life as he knew it. One day he walked into the most significant trouble of his life, though not his own making. Earlier that day, a boy from another gang wandered into their turf. In gangs, this is a no-no, so several of Juan's gang brothers beat him up and stole his bike. Unknowing to Juan, who was on his way home, this kid's brother was seeking revenge. The brother jumped out of an alley from about 20 feet away, seeing Juan and knowing he was a member of the group that beat up his brother; he opened fire. The first shots hit Juan in the leg, but he immediately turned and ran to nearby cars for cover.

Before he has gotten very far, he remembers the third shot's impact, which hit him in the spine. He remembers falling, and when he tried to keep moving, there was no feeling from his legs. He did not know it at that time, but his spine was severely damaged. The gunner left, thinking he had killed Juan. When Juan arrived in the hospital, the doctors put him in a medically induced coma. For several days his mother kept squeezing his hand to make contact hoping he was still alive inside. Finally, Juan awoke and remembered seeing his family surrounding him all in tears, and that sight shook him to his core. He had that realization that he had done a terrible wrong to his family and had hurt them badly. Many of his family had flown in from Puerto Rico to be there and help out. He woke up to the errors of his ways, and the price he paid for his wildness was quite severe. After he had started to heal, he was transferred to a rehab hospital to learn how to live in a new paradigm.

Juan had a mentor assigned to him to help with his transition to this new world of non-accessibility, and it was then he realized he would never walk again. With that mentor's help, he began learning how to use a wheelchair. In addition, the staff urged him to start playing some wheelchair sports. He credits his mentor's can-do attitude and the athletes he played with to awaken his desire to succeed despite the obstacles he faced.

In contrast, his roommate at the Rehab Center, who was also paralyzed, suffered deep depression from losing his mobility. When Juan went home, he found new challenges as his home was not accessible. There were steps and very little room for a wheelchair, and the bathroom was tight for him to maneuver. The family did not have the resources to fix it, so Juan had to make do. Lucky for Juan, he had plenty of support from others in the disability community to keep pushing himself. Juan played basketball and softball, and his friends, who were also disabled, inspired him to finish his education. He had been a freshman in high school, and in those days, high schools were not all accessible, so when he went back, it was to an accessible school. Nothing was simple for him, his home, traveling to a school, and just everyday life, but he was determined to make something of himself.

After graduating high school, he and a roommate lived off the small amount of money that the government gave out, but it was a month-to-month existence. Another friend, also disabled, was given a scholarship to the University of Illinois at Urbana-Champaign. Juan went along for the ride and found an excellent program that showed people with disabilities a chance to compete and focused on giving them an education that he could use to make it in the world. It was an entire environment aimed at providing people a chance to be self-sufficient. He was wowed and applied and started playing wheelchair basketball under coach Mike Frogley (Frog). Frog was a no holds barred got to win coach whose teams were always some of the best and won championships or close behind. One of his teammates was Steve Serio, playing guard for UI. I happened to cover the Wheelchair College Basketball Finals a few years later while working as the Voice of X-Able Sports Website. I called the championship game and watched them win at the University of Oklahoma.

Serio, during a fast break, lost control of his chair and flipped. He came back up and, without any hesitation, proceeded to put the ball in the hoop. I was blown away by that feat. I remember commenting to my listening audience, "don't try that at home." I met Frog and saw his magic and his superb coaching myself. As an aside, another player that I covered in the National Championships. Matt Stock was on the opposing team, had just finished being in a Nike commercial. The commercial was powerful as you see only his upper body talking and bouncing a basketball. He tells you why he did not feel like playing ball that day or why he was not playing well. You know the ones, "a case of the Mondays," I have a headache, it's raining, I am not inspired, my coach hates me, I did not sleep well, or "I have a hot date." After sharing all these excuses, He puts the ball in the hoop, and then you see Matt is in a wheelchair, and he says, "my feet hurt as he wheels away, and you realize he has been in a wheelchair the whole time and has artificial feet." Nike's tagline is "No Excuses," and it's a good one too. Well back to the story of Juan. Juan and Steve ended up in one of coach Frog's practices with their chairs tied together by rope. The challenge was a tug of war against each other. With a big body, Juan was able, despite Serio putting on the brakes to pull him all over the gym for several minutes. Then Frog had them do it again, but this time Juan was tired, and Steve, despite Juan's efforts, reversed the experience, and he dragged Juan around. Now both were exhausted, and their hands were cramping, but the coach had them do it again, and the two, no matter how hard they tried, were unable to budge the other. Juan and Steve tried for several minutes, well beyond anything they had ever done, and showed themselves new levels of strength they did not know they had. Juan remembers this as an 'I did it.' Juan competed with UI for two years but found himself called back to Chicago and entered UI in Chicago. The siren call came from a girl he met who was interning with the Chicago Cubs Wheelchair Softball team. That siren, Maureen, is now his wife and the mother of his three children, Morgan, the eldest, and his twins, Benjamin and McKenna. I had met Juan while covering a wheelchair softball tournament in Chicago earlier, not far from Wrigley Field. My daughter brought Juan over to interview without telling me anything other than he had a great story. He shared his life with its many twists and turns; he proudly told me he would be the first person in his family to graduate from college. After getting his Bachelor's in Human Resource Management, Juan went to work, helping others overcome their physical challenges. Still, Juan did that, which was not enough, so when

his wife finished getting her master's degree, Juan decided it was his turn and went back to get an MBA in Information Technology. Not only did he finish college, but he also ended up with a master's degree that could help him do the work he needed and happily raised a family. Currently, he is a Database Analyst for the Emergency Nurses Association in Schaumburg, Illinois. Juan looks at his life and what it has brought him. Now waking up in the middle of the night after a strenuous evening of playing basketball or softball to feed his twin children might be challenging, but it is one he has taken on with no regrets. He still works to mentor others with disabilities to overcome their obstacles, and he has proven that they are not impossible.

I asked Juan if there is an organization that he feels good about. "I've recently joined the board of the Chicago Adaptive Sports foundation. The founders of this foundation share my beliefs on using sport to show our disabled population that they can succeed despite their limitations. "

https://www.chicagoadaptivesports.com/

Chicago Adaptive Sports is focused on serving the adaptive sports community in the Chicago land area.

We believe sports have the power to equip athletes with the tools to face any challenges, and I think you can see that with Juan's story.

photo: *Rob loading backpacks and shoes for Uperdang Gadi*

chapter 6

BE CAREFUL WHO YOU INVITE TO DINNER

I have taken you into the world of the arts with Thomas Wilkins, and then we visited the disability world, focusing on wheelchair sports. Now I want to bring you deeper into another story in my life. I feel sometimes like I have lived several lives, and I think as you learn about this part and through my own experiences, my gateway to meeting other more amazing human beings. I think you will continue to understand why I had to write this book.

The Chinese bless you by saying, "may you live in interesting times." I would add and travel to strange and exotic locales. For many, Kathmandu in Nepal and Djibouti in Africa would certainly fit that description. These are places that invoke mystery and the unknown. Sometimes I still cannot imagine how that came to be on my list of travel places. So let's start in the beginning. In early November 2007, a very destructive Typhoon came out of the Indian Ocean. Like most of us, I took little notice of that, and since I was living in Florida, hurricanes were always aiming for our state and Tampa Bay, yet the big ones just missed us. Also, how many of us pay attention to disasters in other parts of the world. Little did I know that a typhoon hitting the country of Bangladesh would affect me and be part of a defining moment in my life. That November, my daughter had decided to host Thanksgiving at her new house. I had previously invited some international military officers to experience this wonderful American tradition at my own home. So we combined our Thanksgiving dinner and extended the invite to my international friends. One family that came was Lieutenant Colonel Ataul Hasan, the Senior National Representative from Bangladesh, and the other was Colonel Samuel Alito from Kenya who came with his son. Ataul came with his wife Dina and his two sons. It was a real mixture of cultures. My wife and I were from NY and Jewish. My daughter had married Elio Navarro, whose father was from Spain via Cuba, and his mother from Puerto Rico. This mixing of the two island nations made for a great challenge, who made the best flan, the Puerto Rican vs. the Cuban. This Thanksgiving was a delicious combination of turkey and black beans and rice and other delicacies. That is why America is great that we come from many cultures and yet are willing to share our differences and experiences. Having Bangladesh and Kenya guests just added to the flavors. This successful Thanksgiving joining was the beginning of inviting International Coalition Officers and their families to my house and expanding this to many families in the Tampa Bay community. Over many years over a hundred families or single men or women serving from afar but stationed at CENTCOM participated in Thanksgiving in American homes. The stories that resulted from deep and lasting friendships are something I am proud to have been a part of.

My Bangladeshi friend asked me for help as that Typhoon had severely damaged his country. I think Colonel Hasan was hoping I could raise some money to send there. I had another idea. I met a Buddhist monk from Sri Lanka living in Princeton, New Jersey, who was doing humanitarian work in Kenya and Sri Lanka. Bhante Wimaula visited us for many years, and I organized Buddhist philosophy talks and meditations to share his teachings. We also had him do book signings of 'Lessons from the Lotus: Practical Spiritual Teachings of a Traveling Buddhist Monk'. I immediately thought of him and told the Colonel, and right then, we put through a call to his cell phone.

He was not in Princeton, New Jersey, but answered his call from a Buddhist Temple he oversaw in Kenya. My other guest Colonel Alito also knew Bhante and had helped him distribute wheelchairs for people unable to walk in Kenya. Upon hearing about the disaster, he decided he would investigate and see what we could do. He took a plane to Bangladesh to be met by some of the Colonel's fellow military there. There they arranged transportation to get to the affected area. The most efficient way to tour the disaster area was on the back of a motorcycle when

photo: *Elder from Uperdang Gadi*

he arrived. I vividly remember this Buddhist Monk's pictures in the purple and orange robes traveling on that motorcycle. We had also arranged a truckload of supplies made up of water and clothes for the homeless people as a first step as the people had lost everything. We ended up collaborating on this project, me in Tampa raising the money, and he in Bangladesh. He contracted with various builders to make simple houses, a room, and an outside kitchen to give shelter to these families. The cost was $750 to $1000, depending on which side of the river they were built. Working with the Bangladesh Army, we made fifty homes and three community buildings used as religious houses of worship and community gathering places. I know it was a drop in the bucket in how many people were without homes, but at least these people had homes again, and the community had a meeting place together. Later that year, when Bhante came on one of his visits to Tampa, he was invited by the Bangladesh officers to CENTCOM's international center. He was excited to meet Colonel Hasan in person, and while there, he was invited to share his humanitarian aid experiences. The Nepal Senior officer, Colonel Bharat Gurung, attended the talk and then asked me when we were coming to his country. I remember thinking, what have I got myself into? He mentioned that there were many educational challenges in the remote areas that needed help. After the initial shock, I was intrigued and started thinking about it. It was one thing working in Tampa to help house some people across the world, but this was getting serious! At first, I thought that this would be a partnership with my friend Monk. I also think the satisfaction of helping people was a thrill. I knew I had many international friends from the many years of being connected to the Coalition, playing tennis and golf with some, helping others when they asked, but to devote serious time to this was a big step. Up to that moment, I had always worked at helping my local community. I had served as President of the Board of several organizations. I had created two of those, the Tampa Bay Business Committee for the Arts and the Kaleidoscope Children's Festival, but this was a big step up for me, but it felt right, so I said yes without even talking with it Bhante. When I found out he had other plans that would take up his time, I found myself on my own. Lucky for me, I had made friends at the South Tampa Chamber of Commerce during my time on the Board and serving as President, and a couple of friends with big hearts were willing to join me on this endeavor. Major Prem Pun had replaced Colonel Gurung as the Senior Representative from Nepal, and he was ready to help. His first act was introducing me to a young man, Hemu Adhikari, from Nepal but now living in Tampa. Hemu had been sending books to Nepal inspired by his American son, who was shocked that they had no libraries. He had many friends in the Chitwan area in the south of the country near the Indian border. We met for coffee at a Starbucks, and w e joined forces to help this faraway land. This was the beginning of Global Action Coalition.

photo: *Rob trying Satu at Kirantar School*

chapter 7

I LEARN HOW THE OTHER HALF LIVE

Now I have primed you to take you to far, far away Nepal. I remember my first trip to Nepal vividly. Global Action Coalition was still just a baby, and we had applied for IRS status and were excited to start working there. The plan was to go there by myself and meet up with my partner Hemu in the Chitwan area during my stay. Hemu, you might remember, had been introduced to me by Major Prem Pun, the Senior National Representative from Nepal to CENTCOM. This young Nepalese American had been shipping books to Nepal to help with the education needs where he had grown up. Hemu had grown up in a small village near a roadside town called Tandi. He had dreams for a different life, worked hard to excel at math, and had excellent people skills. His ticket out of Nepal ended him up in Tampa by working in tourism and the hotel industry. Hemu had a gift for finance, and we became a great team.

I knew we shared a desire to make a difference, and he had contacts with friends back there, and my contacts were with the Nepal military. So we decided to meet in Nepal in the Chitwan region to visit a village and get something started. Our plan seemed simple at that time.

I bought the plane ticket, not knowing what I was getting into traveling to a third-world country. Even the financial part was a big deal. I had recently filed for divorce and lived frugally as the art gallery in 2009 was not making a lot of money. Going away for two weeks so far away was scary. Would I have enough money to pay my bills? Would I miss out on making some sales?. All these thoughts kept going through my head. When asked by one of my friends whether I had any fears, I replied that I trusted in the universe's magic to support me. It is a long trip to Nepal by plane. First, you fly to a major US airport, and I flew out of Washington, DC, from Tampa.

After waiting five hours, we boarded the flight to Qatar. That was the longest flight, and sleeping on a plane was never a great experience. Hours later, I found myself with another long layover of about seven hours at Qatar's airport. They have this quiet space with dim lights and reclining chairs for you to close your eyes. You have to be lucky, find one, try to get comfortable, set your alarm, and close your eyes. Finally, I fell asleep only to be woken by the Indian woman near me. She was talking, and people around her were telling her to be quiet, and the more they did, the more she told them to mind their own business. I guess the concept of a 'quiet room' for her was not the same as mine. I wondered how loud she was at home. I was still fatigued when I boarded my flight to Kathmandu. Kathmandu sounded so mystical, so exotic, and so it is, and then so disappointing too. I took a taxi to Thamel, a crazy part of the city with loads of shopping, loads of tourists, loads of noise, and hotels. I felt very alone.

I spent the next day learning how to travel the city by taxi. Everything was a challenge, but I was not going to let that stop me. So I started asking before I engaged the taxi for the next ride what it should cost. The drivers were hoping I was ignorant to overcharge me, seeing I was from another country. The first time in a developing nation without anyone to show me around was a learning experience. That day I went to different agencies to better understand the situation on the ground. One was the World Food Bank offices to learn what they did and what they recommended. In remote Nepal, one of the secrets of getting children to school is to feed them. I found out how true this was when I finally got to the villages in the mountains. Many of the schools had only half of the students attending that were living in the area. These Chepong people, or any others, have lived a subsistence life that had not changed for thousands of years. Education was a foreign idea for many, and they could not see how that would help them get in the crops. Another visit was to meet Mahabir Pun, who was very friendly and helpful. You can read more about him as he has a chapter in this book. I left thinking I was hoping someday to work with him to make this country better. I also went to the Finland Consulate to see what they were doing. Many countries had offices there, and different countries picked projects to support. Finland was concerned with education, hoping to see if we could find a common cause. They said if we ever started working in the West's remotest areas, they would love to talk with us. They told me what they had done to work with the Education Ministry and supply books to schools. I never found any school in Nepal that had those books. I wonder where their books ended up.

I heard stories of people getting sick from food, so I decided to be very careful and be a vegetarian in Nepal. In a third-world country, you have to be cautious about what you eat and drink and how you bathe. The water is usually not safe, so you need to drink bottled water everywhere. Imagine taking a shower and washing your hair and trying to keep the water from entering your mouth, or having to remember that the tap water has not been purified and putting your toothbrush in it. So in my travels to Djibouti, Nepal, and Cuba, I go into safe mode when it comes to drinking water. In Tampa, I had met some of the Nepalese community and eaten one of the counties' delicacies, Momo. Momo is a Nepali pierogi filled with potato, cabbage, paneer (Indian goat cheese), or meats. So I was determined to make my way through the country eating Momo. Another surprise was Chow Mein. I grew up in the US, and Chow Mein was a soupy kind of noodle dish, and I was never in love with it and never ordered it in Chinese restaurants or on the school lunch menu. American Chow Mein was usually tasteless. In Nepal, this was one of the excellent noodle dishes and became another favorite of mine. Of course, Dal Bhat, the lentil dish, and the many vegetables were good too. Right now, as I write this, I am picturing a delicious plate of Momo. Yum.!

So eating was not a hardship. Like many countries worldwide, another challenge in Nepal is the danger on the roads with crazy driving. There are a couple of traffic lights in Kathmandu, but mostly it is a free for all. You will find motorcycles weaving in and out of traffic, along with small tourist vans stopping at a moment's notice. Everybody is trying to get around the small carts with their motors carrying goods. The bravest person receives the right of way. I have driven in New York City, and I would not dare to get behind the wheel of a car in Nepal. Vehicles will pass on a curve blowing their horns on the main highways, which are only two-lane gravel roads winding through the mountains. I will often read of a tourist bus or truck going off the side of a road and think that could have been me. Everyone wore masks to protect them from all the vehicles spewing fumes. I found Kathmandu's streets overfilled with cars, buses, and anything that can use a motor. It is the same in all the small towns and cities there. When I travel, I try to either find an air-conditioned bus and pray the others don't open the windows or rent a van if I am with a group. As I am writing this during the pandemic and with Nepal shut down, I have seen the streets empty, and I wonder what people think about not protecting themselves from traffic but from the virus. I think amidst the challenges and tribulations of this Covid 19 virus, the one positive part is that we have let the planet and ourselves have a moment to breathe fresh air before going back into full pollution mode.

Off I went on a tourist bus. Loud music blaring from the radio turned up high, and the top of the bus filled with the extra luggage and extra passengers clinging to the suitcases. Always there is a young man who hangs out the front door to navigate us through all the road challenges. As I have said, there are no highways as we know them in this country. The main road to Chitwan in the south is sometimes paved and not in good repair. The road snakes from Kathmandu down into the valley and then through the mountains to India's plains.

Nepal is a developing country but with proud and friendly people. A few years before I arrived, they had fought a war with the Maoists. The Maoists, supported by many poor villagers, were fighting a government with a corrupt king. Many of the people had to be careful with their allegiances. One day the Maoist guerrillas would be in the town and take want they needed, and if they thought you had helped the government, you risked being killed as they requisitioned supplies they required. The next day it could be the Army or the Police with the same results. It was a crazy time for Nepal. Finally, they ended the war, and now there is a national government without a king. The military has become mixed from both sides and seems to be working. But for the everyday man, life goes on for many without seeing any fundamental changes. Corruption still is a significant issue, but now both sides are involved.

When I finally arrived after this seven-hour bus ride, I had a snapshot of how the people in rural areas survive. You see many are along the road, small shops selling mostly the same things, foods and water stand side by side. A young girl hopped on the bus on one stretch of road and rode it to the next stop down the mountain to sell water and candy to the passengers. Then she jumped on the next bus going back up the hill. Usually, this child would be in school, but in this subsistence living, everyone supports the family, and the idea of education is not a priority. There are restaurants that the bus drivers all know, and the food is quick and tasty. I remember one time sitting next to tourists from Spain speaking Spanish. It was a funny moment knowing that all the people around me had no idea what we were saying, which was the experience I had been living while there. During my stay, I found myself experiencing a sense of isolation. All around me, people were speaking Nepali, and I so wanted to know what they were saying and wanted to respond. I think we take communication for granted until we experience something like this. When Suzanne and I traveled to foreign countries, it was different because we had each other. I will say I found the people of Nepal so very welcoming and generous. When my tourist bus arrived at the stop in Chitwan, I found Rupendra Karmacharya waiting for me.

Rupendra or Rupen was a childhood friend of Hemu's. To meet him is to fall in love with him. He is a gentle soul who hides a scholarly mind. He has studied the archaeology and sociology of the area. One of his projects dealt with an excavation at the site of Buddha's birth in Lumbini, which is not far from there. He also is a successful entrepreneur. Rupen met with his motorcycle, and we began one of the many travels around the area with me riding on the back. After taking me to a small hotel near the jungle, we met with Hemu, visiting his parents. We picked the Chitwan area for our first project near a wildlife preserve that many tourists visited to see the beautiful jungles filled with tigers, hippos, rhinos, and many exotic animals. Chitwan was where Hemu was born, and he had many friends there who wanted to support us. If you want an incredible experience, you can spend a night in the Tiger Tops. Screened in raised shelters surrounded by jungle and tigers are out there along with much other life. I have not tried that, maybe one day. I did ride the elephants one morning and saw some hippos. While waiting to board the elephant, I was with a group of Chinese tourists. I walked over to the Chinese tour guide to ask her some questions. She said they owned Nepal, and I could understand the presence of this powerful big neighbor to the North.

Meanwhile, India, the southern behemoth, also believes Nepal is theirs too. The only one who disagrees is the Nepali, which has never been conquered, and yet they have to tread lightly amidst the giants. On the north side of the main road, you can head up into the mountains where there are many small villages. Hemu, Rupen, and I planned our next step, a hike to a remote mountain village, Uperdang Gadi, which had an elementary school. Before we headed out on our trek, we stopped by some stores to buy shoes and backpacks to take with us. I was careful to stay out of the negotiations since the stores had two prices, one for the visitors and one for the locals. To get to Gadi, we were going to be traveling all day. First, it was a jeep ride to the stopping-off place. There we met porters from the village to help carry the supplies. They put these straps around their heads to carry these gifts, and then we headed up into the mountains. Hemu also invited some of his friends who wanted to be part of the trip. We crossed many small streams to climb up to the village, taking off our shoes many times. Since it was late October, we did not worry about leaches. After six hours, we reached Uperdang Gadi, a magical place. An old fort guarding the mountain passes lay quietly, waiting for the past soldiers to return. There were a small two-room school and a few houses, and later on, Rupen built a tourist cabin there for hikers. The tourist cabin was Rupen's way of promoting an alternative livelihood for the local people. Most of the children and families live within a couple of miles through up and down trails. I always remember the local Tennesseans bragging about how they walked over the ridges to get to school. Here this was the reality that children faced every day. Along the ridges are terraced areas for growing rice and millet. The school's view is of the valley below with distant lights shining at night, and a different life exists. The lights are a siren lure for many of the children to experience the other life. We were tired after our long hike, and after dinner, several of the girls from the school serenaded us with a traditional welcoming dance. We retired to the loft of a building to get some sleep. It took time in the morning to explore the old earthen fortress before the big ceremony. The beautifully covered grass fort beckoned me. I walked on the walls imagining in this peaceful area soldiers on guard. Before we could present the shoes and backpacks, the villagers thanked us profusely in only the way people in remote areas can. They covered us with leis and marked us with tika, a red powder. This ceremony is an exceptional event, and you can feel the love from everyone. I have experienced this many times on my trips to Nepal, and each time I have felt undeserving of this honor, I have understood there are times we need to be gracious and let others give to us. Next, we had the children line up, and we handed them the gifts plus books a friend of Hemu had brought. Watching them receive these items was terrific compared to the jaded response we mostly see back at home. The boys and girls wouldn't take off the backpacks. Next came a show from the children of music and dance, and before long, Hemu, Rupen, and his friends and I were whirling and dancing with the children and adults. Finally, we had ourselves another simple meal of Dal Bhat from our hosts. I then learned another lesson from Rupen. I tried to give our hosts some money for the meals, and they refused to accept it. I told Rupen, and he said that this is their custom to give food freely and lodging. No matter that, by their generosity, they may run out of food later. The way to not shame them was to leave some money for them to find.

Years later, when visiting one of our village schools, I had the opportunity to visit the classrooms and eat lunch with the children afterward. We had started many lunch programs in many villages to feed the children; the first was at Uperdang Gadi. I was surprised that in the 5th-grade class, there was a child around five years old sitting quietly. I asked the teacher, and she explained that the family had run out of food. When the parents headed into the jungle or forest to forage for edible roots and other foods, the responsibility for taking care of the youngest fell on the oldest. Before we had started the lunch program, the children would just miss school. Once we started feeding the children at the school, they would bring their brother or sister. The teacher was worried that I would not like feeding these other mouths. I was glad for the young ones to experience school. In the Chepong villages, education was not important to many of the parents. They had not gone to school, and they lived a subsistence life where education did not help them harvest the rice and millet. They had lived that way for thousands of years, and the only way to entice them to send their children to school was to feed them lunch. Many children had only two meals a day, and sometimes they only got one when the food was running out. On this last trip to the Kirantar school to see our Satu lunch program in operation, Satu mixed local grains and some sugar. It required adding water, and most children would do that and sit down with their friends as you would expect. Some of the children were mixing it up and immediately eating it while still standing. They did this because of how hungry they were, and this lunch meal was the first meal of the day. I had never seen children with this kind of hunger

photo: *At Kirantar lunchtime*

before. This was not that I have to have an oreo cookie or Good Humor Bar hunger. This was so primal, and I understood why the children were always so short and skinny. I have told this to many American children in our Sister School Program. As you can see, I learned so much by being on the ground and keeping my eyes and ears open to the issues they faced.

I was touched and amazed at the challenges these people faced. They had no safety net, and yet they lived their lives with a grace that I found profound.

I also learned that when you fixed one problem, you created another. We found the lunch program would often double the attendance, and then the schools would be overwhelmed by the new students of various ages starting at the beginning. It was impossible to get more teachers from the government, so we had to hire them ourselves. We kept adding new classrooms in another area as the students in the area now needed a middle school. We also found that during the winter, cold affected attendance, so we started a sweater program. I often reflect on differences that the children experience there versus what our children do here. So as you see, I have become this expert on 3rd world education the hard way, one step at a time. I have also been transformed by my time above the jungles of Chitwan, and I want to share a poem I wrote in my lame attempt to share my experience.

UPERDANG GADI

(Dedicated to Rupen Karmacharya)

Far away, where
the city lights twinkle
In the distant panorama
we visit a people almost forgotten

There is no government here
no care for kings and presidents
Buildings fall and rock the world
but no echo is felt here
Like and Incan City
clinging to the mountain tops
Uperdang Gadi
beautiful in its living crown
Atop sits a stone fortress
guarding ancient routes to
kingdoms far below
Sleeping peacefully forgotten

Life is simple up here
but is there enough food?
From small patches of rice
to feed the children?

We visitors from below
carrying things so basic
Yet we are the Gods
with our puny gifts

Who would think

backpacks and shoes
would brings such joy to children
surely not in America

We are fed simple meals
rich in flavors foreign to our palates
yet served with such love
that bridges our hearts

We who are the givers end up the given
touched by their warmth
Are we truly not the same?
No we are changed forever

Rob Rowen, November 2009

photo: *We love the children and it is returned*

photo: *Mahabir visits Clemson to talk innovation*

chapter 8
MAHABIR PUN

*A Man With
No Small Mission*

My work with Global Action Coalition sometimes connects with my being Chair of the World Affairs Council Upstate in Greenville, SC. I will tell how they intersected in this story, and it turned out to be an amazing experience. I had heard that Mahabir Pun from Nepal was traveling around the US and Canada. Why was that a big deal for me? That is the story I have to tell. I started working to have us included in his travels and stop in the Upstate of South Carolina. You might remember from the last story I had met Mahabir when I first traveled to Nepal. At that time, I knew he was working on creating Wireless Nepal, ensuring everyone in the country had access to the future. I had taken time out in Kathmandu to find his offices and visit him. I was new to the humanitarian aid business and had no real idea of what I was to face there, so every opportunity to learn about the challenges there was worth doing. Among his projects, besides working to bring wireless to remote mountain villages, he was trying to distribute small, almost unbreakable mini computers to elementary schools in remote communities that could run on solar power and battery. I was very impressed with his vision and hoped one day to partner with him in our projects. Now fast forward to 2018, nine years later, and this national hero in Nepal was on a fifty-plus-day tour of the US and Canada. In most of the North American cities, it was Nepalese people he was meeting. They had moved here to get an education, and many stayed to work and live here (this is often called the Nepalese Diaspora). I realized this was an incredible opportunity to bring this person to our area, so I contacted him and scheduled meetings at Clemson University and the University of South Carolina Upstate, plus a visit to Greenville. It was one of the few places that a non-Nepalese person at the airport met him. I enjoyed bringing this simple, dedicated man to the universities and watching him inspire the students and faculty with his. focus. Mahabir had an underlying message: his life's focus on helping his country through innovation spurring economic growth. Nepal is a developing country sandwiched between two giants, India and China. People who have left Nepal understand why this country needs new answers to survive and compete globally. He raised money from the Nepalese living in the US, and more important was his call for innovators to join him in his work. So how did he get on this quest? His story is compelling. It starts with him graduating from High School and becoming a teacher. Mahabir wanted more, and he knew he needed a better education. He searched for grants to go to America to further his studies. Mahabir ended up at the University of Nebraska in Kearney at 33 as an undergraduate student. There he impressed the professors as they polished him. Mahabir also realized finding a job with his skills in his home country would be a challenge. He decided to return anyway, dedicated to making change happen. His professors at the University of Nebraska Kearney and others in the community were so impressed with his dedication that they started a fund to support his work in Nepal. He said at that time, "I knew nothing about development back then, but I wanted to do something." When he returned to his town, his community asked him to build a high school. Students in Nepal graduating from their middle school sometimes have considerable distances to travel to the high schools. For them, this is usually the end of their educational opportunities. It is hard to get government support to create a new school in Nepal, so you have to find the land, build the school, and prove you can support it before they send teachers. So Mahabir gathered the support and oversaw the completion of the school. Then he realized his next task would be to create sustainability to pay for that and other necessary improvements to keep the school going. Some of his ideas that have ended up supporting the school were, starting a yak farm for milk and cheese, handmade papermaking, and creating community-managed hiking trails and zero carbon emission lodges with water-powered electricity in the mountains. Both of these were wildly successful and showed him that innovation would be the key to the entire country's success. His Wireless Nepal organization was responsible for bringing internet capability to 150 villages and schools where previously there was nothing. These actions paved the way for his decision to create the National Innovation Center of Nepal. *"It took me a long time, but I realized that all of this community work, important as it was, was just scratching the surface and was not enough to make Nepal an economically prosperous nation. We will never rebalance our huge trade deficit until and unless we build a culture of innovation and investing in innovation. That is the ultimate growth engine"*. I was excited to bring him here. I found that his quest for innovation and his willingness to work with anyone created excitement at the Watt Family Innovation Center at Clemson and the George Dean Johnson College of Business at USC Upstate. We are continually working to develop

long-distance partnerships. Another connection we made was a retired senior US military officer is working to find used obsolete microwave equipment to complete a country-wide wireless network in remote mountain villages. One of the interesting things I noticed was the element of surprise on everyone to his dedication and resolved to work tirelessly to help his country. His visit was the 43rd in about 50 days. He took no time for sightseeing and used his spare time to plan for his next city visit or follow up on a previous connection. Mahabir Pun has been working for the last 27 years in Nepal without a salary. The community and his friends have supported him for all his needs. He lives a frugal life focused in a way that is both inspiring and amazing. At that time, the National Innovation Center for Nepal had 30 major projects. Some of the work was with solar and thermal power, e-commerce, medical drones, baby warmer m ginger soft drinks, conversion of used vehicles to electric vehicles, electronic health recording systems, a portable storage mechanism for extending the shelf-life of horticultural produce, and alternative protein sources for poultry farming. When the Covid-19 hit Nepal, he started making and distributing ten different items to help mitigate the spread of the Covid-19 virus, including fixing used respirators and developing new models made in Nepal. The items include PPE, Swab collection booth, aerosol box, UV disinfection box, nasal swab, nursing robot, face shield, and sanitizer dispenser. The Innovation Center is collaborating with the researchers of Stanford University, University of California San Francisco, the University of California Berkeley to develop a ventilator, fabric for a mask, Pneumask, and PAPR (powered air-purifying respirator). You can check out their website, which is always changing and wildly innovative (https://nicnepal.org/). One interesting thing I learned about Mahabir. This wide range of activities won him many international accolades and made most people rest on their laurels. But, and here is the kicker, this was not enough for Mahabir. He put all his medals and trophies up for auction on Facebook and made available his own land to finance his new project, a National Innovation Center for Nepal. What about long-term sustainability? "The Center is not a charity, and I am determined for it to be self-sustained over time. This is why I don't ask people for money upfront — I ask for their expertise and mentoring first and foremost. If the plan is good, the money will follow. I also tell people that I only accept one-off donations. Mahabir is open to new ideas and collaboration with individuals and institutions from around the world. If interested, you may contact him at mahabir@nicnepal.org.

FEB 1964

photo: *Temple Hayes*

chapter 9

REVEREND
TEMPLE HAYES

*There Is A Difference Between
Being Born And Being Birthed*

So far in this journey about Defining Moments, we have visited with a conductor of orchestras, wheelchair sports, and its heroes and Nepal and my life with the exciting people I have met. Now I want to share someone who has made a difference in my life, and her story is compelling in another way. We start this journey in Spartanburg, South Carolina, not far from where I currently reside.

We have heard people saying they were 'called' to do something. These people listened to an inner voice that told them there was something they had to do. This next story is about someone who had that calling but also had many challenges along the way. Temple Hayes was born at the wrong time in the wrong place, which created a deep painful sense of separation. Let us journey with her as she meets those challenges and finds real joy, inner peace, and happiness. I think you will find this story compelling and inspirational and, indeed, for some, an inspiration to a challenge.

Temple Hayes, at five years old, had a calling to spiritual life and the creator. She had a sense she would bring change to the world. Was this a curse, or was it a blessing to have? She knew things more eastern in spiritual beliefs but was born to a deep-rooted Baptist community in the pre-Google internet age, where her ideas were not seen anywhere or even whispered. She was an overachiever, President of the Student Council, played two instruments, and was also a high school mascot. In the eyes of her community, accomplishing all that in her rural South Carolina area at most, she could be a guidance counselor or perhaps a PE teacher.

Her beliefs and intuitive understanding found that she was not attracted to the norm; marrying a man and raising children did not interest her and was not what the community expected. At thirteen, she found herself attracted to the same sex, a major taboo in the church she grew up in. When she shared this with her Grandmother, her response was to say I love you, but I won't see you in heaven. That hurt her badly. In discovering she was a lesbian, she started to explore her identity. When she was thirteen, she met a seventeen-year-old girl and began a relationship; her family was shocked. Her uncle thought it would work itself out, but her family flipped out. They were a well-known family in Anderson, SC., so she was taken for mental health assessment. In those days, as it still is in some rural communities, she would have been taken away to a place to undergo a re-education to come back to Jesus. So she lied and hid her sexual identity and also her spiritual questioning. She even began to believe that she, as a fourteen-year-old, was going to go to hell.

Her community rejected her, and that was so very destructive to her inner soul. In response, she abandoned and sabotaged herself with extreme partying and doing crazy things. She started drinking, and even though her body told her to stop, knowing that it was poison to her, she kept it up. In her time in South Carolina, she had twelve to fourteen car accidents, of which four could have easily killed her and totaled at least two cars. She was jailed twice and should have died in one of those accidents. She was a danger to her community and herself. Yet Temple learned to become successful in hiding her destructive side. This student was a top All-American softball player and student with good grades enrolled at Winthrop College, aimlessly heading to destruction. One thing that helped her was having a cyst removed. This medical procedure delayed her first semester in college, and she ended up working at the Michelin tire plant in Greenville, SC. At this time, she met Don Bliss, who she thought was only interested in her because he wanted to sleep with her. He told her as he got to know her that she had a gift to be a teacher. Don awakened in her an early belief that she had hidden deep down and knew he was telling her the truth. I got to meet Don and asked him about meeting Temple. He said she was a line worker at the tire plant, and he was her supervisor. He knew from the first that she was different and was amazed how every day she came to work with an exuberance not usually found in this kind of work. She put her all into it, and it was a pleasure to have her working there. He invited her to a Unity Church that he belonged to, and she went. She is not sure why she announced to the Unity Minister that she might be gay. Temple was surprised that her statement did not faze the Minister. The response was, "no problem, everyone is accepted here," astounded her. So it was then that her spiritual journey was reborn. She read everything she could find and listened to everything available. She wanted to understand what it meant to be spiritual. Since age fourteen years, this was what she had wanted for herself. She applied to Unity School but was not accepted, so she moved to Fort Lauderdale and enrolled to become a Science of Mind Minister at twenty-seven. You would be surprised to know she still carried her alcoholic addiction with her and was a total recluse each night drinking a bottle of wine. Temple was at war within herself, a person who was having blackouts and searching for the answers to happiness. One day she awoke, and she realized she could not ever drink again. Her inner voice finally won out, and from that day forward has never taken another drink. (34 years at the time of this reading). After serving two communities, she relocated to St. Petersburg, Florida, serving at a Science of Mind Church. She was becoming recognized for her distinct voice and wisdom, and she started speaking around in other communities and churches. Reverend Alan Rowbotham was at the time the Spiritual Leader at First Unity of St. Petersburg. He invited her to speak there as a guest minister and found that the Unity community loved her. He decided he wanted her to be his Associate Minister and convinced her this was where she needed to be. On July 13th, 2003, she took the Assistant Minister's job, and in two years, she would become the Spiritual Leader. As the Lead Minister at First Unity Spiritual Campus of St. Petersburg, Temple has used what she learned to overcome challenges that almost brought her down to be a shining light to many. Her work is Global. She credits the challenges of overcoming her addiction to alcohol and understanding the power that her strict Southern-Baptist upbringing created such chaos in her life as her successes. Temple uses them to help others facing the mountains in their lives. Her teachings state we are all co-creators with God; as long as you keep God in the closet, God is unseen in ways that matter in our lives, and we need to work from love to make a change in our lives. I met Temple in 2009 while going through a divorce. I felt guilty for choosing to be happy and knowing that meant pain for someone else. I was challenged by going to a Church as I grew up Jewish. What I found in the Unity movement was that it wasn't about religion but actively working on your spiritual path and choosing love and forgiveness. I have seen Temple repeatedly lecture and observe how many people believed that she was talking directly to them. Many members of the St. Petersburg campus have been able to deal with challenging issues and find happiness. You can tell a tree by its fruit.

She is an internationally known motivational speaker, a difference-maker, and a proponent for world peace. You can learn more about her at http://www.templehayes.com.

She is also the Founder of www.illli.org -The Institute for Leadership and Lifelong Learning, International.

photo: *Temple speaking at a Seminar*

photo: *Ramjee feeding the Covid hungry*

chapter 10

RAMJEE ADHIKARI

*Somebody Had
To Do It*

I wanted to break up the stories, so I thought Temple's story would change the flavor a bit. So I hope you are ready to journey back to Nepal to meet Ramjee. As it is said in the Bible, "You can tell a tree by it's fruit". Ramjee is one of those human beings who shows up that God's true servants appear in all places and all religions. So see if you agree.

Service as the way to God for many is a great idea but something a little too challenging. I wonder if Ramjee if he ever thought he would ever have to walk the walk. His life was the typical college life in Nepal, many hours from Kathmandu. He was studying Management with plans to start a successful business. He was in a Motivation class. He had that day done his talk on the concept 'Service as the way to know God' when driving back on the roads in the Chitwan area he lived, and again he was amazed that there were so many helpless people along the side of the roads. Some were beggars, and some were just pitiful damaged people with nowhere to go. Remembering the motivational speech, he saw things differently and became emotionally moved. He no longer wondered why no one was helping these people but why he did not help them. Merely handing over bits of change would not resolve solve their hardships. He gathered his friends and family to do something. That something was a picnic. Using local police and friends, they gathered the homeless and brought them to a house. The people they picked up were a collection of life. Some were elderly and sick; some were women who had been severely sexually abused; there were children and some people with mental illness. Some were frightened and resisted, so they were glad to have the police pick them up. When they arrived at the house, the volunteers bathed them, cut their hair, and gave them new clothes before feeding them. I am sure this was a challenging task, and yet for these lost souls, a reprieve from the hell of their lives. Afterward, they returned them to their point of origin. That was the toughest part, and Ramjee could not sleep that night. It went round and round in his mind. All he could think about how unfair it was to give them a taste of another world of love and being taken care of and then lose it. Determined to do something, he and his friends created the Human Service Home. They started with five of the homeless at a house at Sano Pokhara. He called it the Ashram, which means a place of spiritual retreat. It kept growing, children on the street, older adults, primarily women, and many mental disorders. When I visited the Ashram, a woman had been badly sexually abused to the point of death. A child came from that horrifying experience that had left her unable to raise the child. I was moved by the community making a loving home for this almost orphan. I told this story to First Unity Church of St. Petersburg, and they donated money to support this child. The local people at that time supported the Ashram, giving a fistful of rice each day to help feed them. They had many homeless who were dying, and now they had a place to pass with dignity. These were emotional times for the volunteers facing these damaged human beings; it was almost unimaginable. There were good memories as well as some of the homeless were able to be rehabilitated and returned to their homes and families. In Nepal, few families understood mental disorders, and they had no idea what to do. Many live on the edge of poverty, and when a family gets seriously ill, it is a considerable strain on their resources and survival. Ramjee remembers the first twenty he sent back home, and it strengthened his resolve. I first met Ramjee

in 2012. I had no idea what to expect. I found a place filled with people living peacefully. Some were still living in their own worlds, but they were fed and clean and loved. My partner in starting this non-profit organization was Hemu Adhikari. Hemu's was a great partner, and he brought two things to our projects. He worked in the financial world and understood budgets and money issues, and he was from the area in Nepal that we were working. We had a strong comfortability in our relationship that, as I shared earlier, came from traveling together in his country. I trusted him, and he did the same for me. He had told me of our working with Ramjee, and on my next trip to Nepal, I went to see what he was doing. Hemu's matter-of-fact belief that this was a good project did not paint the picture of what I saw. He was right about the need to support Ramjee, but here is where my gift in telling these stories would be necessary to our finding aid. To be successful in finding donors you need to bring them with you on the journey. If not in reality, then in pictures and images that open hearts. Here I am right now doing that and telling his story and what he and his friends were doing to change their neighborhood. Ramjee, with his quiet but magnetic personality, has galvanized amazing support since I visited him.

In 2020, there are now seventeen centers serving one thousand one hundred people. Sixty percent of them are mentally ill, and fifteen percent are children, orphans. He and his group have rehabilitated seven hundred and assisted four hundred leave this world peacefully and with dignity. Kushi, age four, the child of a woman who was gang-raped and left for dead, is starting nursery school. The mother is much better and still getting treatment but unable to raise her child alone fully. Kushi is for Ramjee, the father of a four-year-old this child represents more than just one little girl, but it personally touches him. He says they medicate, meditate, and motivate and counsel the families to help these people better.

I think you can understand and know why this motivator has taught us all that "Service is truly the way to God."

Since I started writing this, I have worked with Ramjee and his staff. Covid-19 has affected many in Nepal. Like many countries, It has shut down businesses and all travel. Many people without work were now living in the streets, unable to get home or make money. We have partnered with him to feed four hundred people during this crisis. His staff was operating food trucks and going each day to different towns and small cities to feed these people. The photographs are heart-wrenching. Nepal is a country with no safety net. The government is lacking, and this is a huge challenge to deal with these kinds of issues. In Nepal, more people during this time died from starvation than COVID. If you want to share your love and support with Ramjee and Mansewa Ashram, you can send your donations to Global Action Coalition (www.globalactioncoalition.org). All of your contributions will go to them, and you will get a receipt from them.

photo: *This little girl was born at Manaswewa*

ROB ROWEN - BANNED STARBUCKS CUSTOMER
STARBUCKS BANS MAN FOR DEFENDING HANDICAPPED 80° 11:01 *WTSP*
BOMB FUSE FOUND   **GETTING TRUMPED**   **WILDFIRE NEAR NAPA**

chapter 11

I AM BANNED
FOR LIFE
FROM STARBUCKS
FOR THREE DAYS

I had to find a place to talk about this strange experience. It is part of my story, and one that I feel fits in with parts of my life that I am sharing. This is a great story.

Somewhere in all these tales, there is an expression coined by Andy Warhol, "in the future, everyone will be world-famous for 15 minutes." I had my fifteen minutes, but it ended up more like three days of fame. Sometimes to be in the news, this 'fame' is more like infamy when they catch you crossing the line of ethical actions, and your mistakes are laid bare to the world. For example, the Congressman caught skinny dipping or another in a meeting in his boxer shorts, here fifteen minutes seemed like an eternity. Mine is a much more exciting story. Where do I begin?. I have to confess I have a weakness for a mocha. Mochas are coffee drinks with chocolate added. For me, it has to be decaf; I take mine with skim or 1% percent milk so I can enjoy that dollop of whip cream on the top. I usually would stop for one at this Starbucks near my art gallery on my way to work. Occasionally I would get my café con Leche fix. Now, remember I have a son-in-law in a power wheelchair, and when he was still driving his van, I would see him hurrying down the parking aisles hoping someone would not back over him. The reason was all the accessible spaces at the shopping mall were taken. Many misuse the placards, not needing them anymore because they are now well or belong to a family member since passed. That is a discussion for another time. What bothers me the most are those that just don't even care and park illegally. This is where we begin our story. This story takes place at the Starbucks I most used on South Dale Mabry and Azeele Ave. in Tampa. This particular one is in a small strip center with only one accessible parking space (some call it handicapped). Still, Ben Ritter, my former Marine friend in a wheelchair, says it is not acceptable anymore).

I could not help to notice some were routinely misusing this space. The excuse I heard most often was, "I am just running in." For my friends in wheelchairs who needed that parking space, there is no running, and if there is one space and it is occupied, they drive on. I later learned to appreciate having spaces reserved when my Mom broke her hip and could barely walk. We do not understand something like this until it directly affects us. I started noticing people with no handicap plate or placard parking in this one space. I would politely ask them to move their car because space was reserved for someone who needed it. Most people would just move their car, but some would give me the finger or say, "who do you think you are, the police?". I tried calling the Police, but rarely would a patrol car answer that call in under 30 minutes, and by then the miscreants were long gone. One time a man claimed I harassed him. I did, but I will let you be the judge. I told him if he didn't move, I would follow him into the store and tell everyone what he did and embarrass him. The Baristas loved me for doing this. They were prohibited from saying anything, partly Starbucks policy and partly by the Store Manager Carla. She told me I should stop harassing 'her customers.' Somehow I was now not one of her customers. One time I came upon a lady sitting in that one valuable parking spot on her phone. I walked over and tapped on her window. When she looked up, I pointed to the sign right before her and asked her to move. I still cannot understand why she thought parking in that space to talk on her phone was ok. Her response was to give me the finger. So, I walked behind her car and, with my I-phone took a picture. I made sure to get her car with her license plate and the sign designating it illegal for her to be there. She got angry and got out of her car, yelling at me and said I was harassing her. Funny how much of a harasser I had become! She said she was calling the Police; I said fine. She did, and so did I. This time, two cars showed up quickly. At first, the woman police officer seemed angry at me and told me to stay by car. I guess she assumed I was the criminal. Then the store manager came out and added her two cents, explaining how evil I was. I finally got to make my statement to the other police car officers, and it got it sorted out. The stupid lady had not bothered to move her car, so they gave her a ticket for illegally parking. I went into the Starbucks; the manager was back in her office, probably happy having said her piece, and the Barista had my mocha ready and then refused to take payment. I walked over to my car, and as I overheard the 'complainant' arguing that they were letting me escape as they were writing her that $250 ticket. Shortly after this incident, the Store Manager told me I was no longer allowed to come into her store, and she would have me arrested for trespassing if I did. So I did what most anyone would do, I tried to go over her head to Corporate Starbucks. That is like trying to talk to God, and all roads lead to the Regional manager. We had what I thought was a good conversation, and he understood my frustration. Then he said before I could go back, I had to stop harassing the customers. I asked him what about the elderly or in a wheelchair or not healthy needed to park in that space. Who is standing up for them? I thought we had finished and he would look into some solutions, but to my surprise, I got a letter from Corporate Starbucks a week later. I figured it would ask me if I had gotten satisfaction for my issue, was I ever wrong. It said that Rob Rowen was now banned from entering any Starbucks in the continental United States. WOW! I could not believe it, so I did what any person in this day and age would do, photographed this announcement, and put it on FaceBook. It was Thursday afternoon, and it did not take long for this to go viral. A couple of hours later, I was on my way home to St. Petersburg when I got a call from Mike Deeson, an investigative reporter and a friend at Channel 10 News. He asked why I had not called him when this happened. I said it was a busy day, and I was still shocked by their response. He then put me on the phone with his Program manager, who wanted to know they send a news team to interview me. They arrived at my home, and I calmly told my side of the story. I guess I came across as very credible, and the next thing I see is the news about a Tampa Bay man banned for life from Starbucks is now on TV and in many newspapers in over 20 cities in the US. Channel 10 is a Gannet affiliate, and they picked it up everywhere. Soon the other local TV news showed up at Nuance Galleries, my business, to interview this celebrity who dared take on Starbucks and got slapped in the face for it. They loved the tagline that "I was standing up for those that couldn't." The next morning, My brother sent me a photo of him standing in front of a Starbucks on Madison Avenue in NYC. He told me they had refused to serve him, they now had facial recognition scanners, and he was a 65% match from the most wanted outlaw in Starbucks history. This is an example of some Rowen family humor. On Saturday morning, when I went to my iPad to see the national news, I found myself on CNN, one of the main stories. They had picked that up from Bay News 9, a local TV channel, and the result was getting phone calls, emails, and messages on my Facebook page. The supporting responses were from all over the country and even Australia, Canada, and the Netherlands. The now-defunct Tampa Tribune's Steve Otto called me a true American folk hero; I will be honest, coming from him was an honor, and I loved that. I remember having conversations with people from other states who had issues about parking at Starbucks, telling me their owns challenges. One was a veteran from Afghanistan who lost a leg there. He said he has watched people walk out of Starbucks and see him waiting for that space needing to use the parking ramp to get out of his vehicle. They realize what they had done and acknowledged it with a sheepish grin. Another man said that his two daughters were born with physical difficulties that required them to live in power chairs. The highlight of their day was their visits to Starbucks for their frappucinos. Many times the one space was taken by people who did not need them. They and many others thanked me profusely. By Sunday, it was big-big news, and I was being interviewed on Skype for ABC World News Tonight by John Bentley. I remembered that I had watched John interview people, never thinking someday it would be my turn. Through this process of being interviewed, when they asked Starbucks for a comment, they said I would be allowed back when I stopped harassing the customers. The watchers saw that I was not a 'serial harasser' but a concerned citizen protecting others' rights. The World News Tonight interview was to run that Sunday night, and about 2 pm, I got a call from a number I did not recognize from Texas. I did not answer and instead listened to the message. It was the Southern Vice President of Starbucks. I figured I would speak to him after the show had run, not wanting to let them off the hook so easily. When I watched it, I found out I was now officially welcomed back to Starbucks. The story does not end there. Another funny and strange part of this story occurred. The Vice President of Florida Starbucks wanted to meet me and discuss the issue. I had developed a friendship with the original news crew from Channel 10, and when they asked how it was going, I mentioned this meeting, not thinking they were going to show up, but they did. Carlos, the VP, got very upset when he saw them in the parking lot and walked around for 10 minutes on his phone, gesturing angrily. I think he was on the phone with somebody up the chain of command, and he was unprepared to talk to the media. Finally, he came in after refusing to answer the reporter's questions. We sat down for a half-hour and talked. I had some great ideas for him. One was better signage, including something in their stores asking their customers to respect the parking space reserved for those that needed it. I also thought some training for store managers would help understand the needs of those customers dealing with physical challenges. Finally, I suggested they offer one afternoon a free latte for anyone with a disability. This idea would have been a good PR move, and many who would come in probably would not be alone, and their friend would also buy a drink. Carlos didn't like my ideas and came back with a meeting with local managers and maybe some free coffee. Well, it was not about free coffee for me, and so that was pretty lame. So he walked out without much agreement and guess who is still waiting outside?. Like the married Congressman who got caught skinny dipping with his girlfriend in the fountain in Washington DC, Carlos did a great impersonation by refusing to talk to the news reporter. He could have said an inane comment that we were trying to find some agreements. Instead, he walked away silently, and they like sharks smelling blood in the water, followed by asking more and more questions. Then he started to run, and so did the reporter and cameraman. It was hysterical watching him chased around the IHOP restaurant building that shared my parking lot, followed by a running reporter and cameraman closely behind.

He managed to make it around the building and back into Nuance Galleries before the TV crew could catch up. I felt bad for him. I also think he believed I set him up, but I hadn't. Coming out of the IHOP in a wheelchair was a boy with his grandma. I knew him; Jimmy also had Muscular Dystrophy like my son-in-law. The News reporter and cameraman, and I went over to interview him, and I asked him would he like to meet Carlos, who was hiding in my building. When Carlos saw them coming, he slipped out the back refusing to face this challenge. We did get a few excellent insights from Jimmy on camera to add to this surreal event. Some last thoughts. In the last few years, Starbucks faced a scandal when two black men were arrested in Philadelphia while waiting for a friend. Another black eye for Starbucks, but they had learned their lesson to respond quickly, not to let these things have a life of their own. I hope you enjoyed this story, and you will be happy to know Carla, the store manager, left shortly after to find work in another field. As for me, you will rarely find me in a Starbucks. Not that I hold any grudge because I appreciate that this happened. It gave many people who watched the news a chance to understand better the challenges people face when it comes to accessibility. Starbucks is one of the more conscious large chains and has a better than average corporate culture for doing good. I find myself more attracted to small coffee shops, and in Greenville, South Carolina, you can find me at Coffee Underground or among some of the other special small coffee roasters. In St. Petersburg, I have always appreciated Black Crow Coffee and Kahwa coffee.

If you find yourself a parking space vigilante like me, there is an answer out there. Parking Mobility, based in San Antonio, Texas, has developed an app for your phone. Easy to use three quick photos, and the GPS button will send the offending driver's info to their headquarters. It only works if your city has signed up. They will issue a ticket and give them a chance to go through an online class to understand the errors of their ways better. It is a non-profit organization, and you can advocate with their help for your city to sign up. It pays for itself, and in San Antonio, Texas, it has cut the number of tickets by 70%. Most tickets are given out at the beginning of the university school year and when parents visit. Mack Marsh, who is the Project Director, is himself in a wheelchair. He tells of being at a music festival, and when he arrived back at his van on a hot day, he found somebody had parked in the ramp zone next to it. He could not get into the van, and he ended up getting severely dehydrated and had to go to the hospital. So the issue of parking can be a serious business. If you live in a community where this is a major problem, I would recommend contacting Mack and learning about their work and how you can protect those needing accessible parking. https://www.parkingmobility.com/

photo: *Peter in his helicopter while in Belgian Air Force*

chapter 12

PETER VAN DEN BROUCKE

Redefining What it Means
to be a Warrior

The building blocks of my story lead me to the next of my amazing superheroes.

This is the story of one of my dearest friends. I met Peter when he served as Belgium's representative to CENTCOM, and I was immediately attracted to his good humor and sensibility. Meeting his wife Dominique was an added plus as she was beginning her journey exploring health and spiritual alternatives. It was also a time for me at the real beginning of my new life with my soon-to-be wife, Suzanne, and we all became close friends. Peter was a Lt. Colonel in their Air Force and took his position at CENTCOM seriously. He asked the hard questions to all, both the American military that was reluctant to give up any information to their allies and the other nations serving there. His good humor and intelligence, combined with a desire to learn what was important, disarmed everyone and led to him becoming a leader in the Coalition, even though he was from such a small country.

So let's go back in time and see what transformed this man from warrior to humanitarian. We should start with his past to understand why he is in the book through the challenges he faced serving in different hot spots in the world. If you ask Peter, he still considers himself a warrior. He believes that true warriors work from the heart and let the mind follow the heart. The heart is always right. And that is the life worth living for, and he has kept to that all his career.

His first operational assignment was in 1994, during the Rwanda crisis. "I was in Brussels, operating the 'family telephone Lines' where families could call to get information about their relatives in Rwanda during the genocide. I have been listening for three days to crying mothers and irate fathers about the lack of political decisions and the lack of means with which the UN mission in Rwanda was performing the Peacekeeping mission. Thousands were dying in front of our eyes, and we were powerless to interfere. The UN has a very tightly focused directive. It gives the military when they arrive in these missions. The use of weapons is by troops in these conflict areas frustrating for those on the ground. Rwanda is a prime example of UN soldiers not saving unarmed Tutsi from being massacred by the Hutus.

Peter realized then that a mission's political responsibilities will always be blamed on the military if they fail. This understanding that in trying to heal a nation, there needs to be a connected effort between the military, the diplomats, the non-profits working on the ground and must include the locals and their cultural needs. Peter found himself on an intense learning curve. At this time in his life, he was newly married with two young sons. His concerns were how he could have a better life for himself, and here he saw many horrors and unable to act. He was looking for that normal man's life, buying a home with all those comforts that come with more money and a career. Peter also had begun understanding how much he had to learn. He likens his path to Alice's taking the other pill, like in Wonderland. Instead of a safe career, he started looking for more overseas assignments and being more effective.

In Bosnia, in 1997, Peter found himself in which had been through a horrible war with its neighbors Serbia and Croatia. This war resulted from the breakup of Yugoslavia. Unleashing old ethnic rivalries, and there were many atrocities. Many countries were sending peacekeeping forces to try to bring a sense of normalcy back.

Bosnia was a brutal place to live. Peter wondered why so many women in prostitution in Europe were from the Balkans countries. One day, he asked a representative of the UN so he could understand what he was seeing. "Well, what is the last thing you can do when you have nothing left? You can sell your daughter, or you can decide yourself to sell your own body". That was happening in Europe; many young women were victims of criminal gangs and had to go into prostitution to survive. Parents even sold children for food to save their siblings.

Bosnia was a war zone at its worst. They were raping young women to destroy the community and family structures. A woman raped is considered damaged, and the children from that cruel act usually had no place where they fit. Peter says, "It was my first shock with the reality of war, and I saw it right in front of my face." Despite the horrors he saw, he started wanting to do what he could to fix it, knowing only small steps were possible.

His next posting was to Kinshasa in what is known as the Congo Democratic Republic in 2004. Peter found himself deployed with the Congolese military staff as a Belgian liaison officer. Here he learned the Western training did not prepare him for the realities of a 3rd world country. The Congo was a place with poor infrastructure, a former colony that the West has abandoned after it took up its independence. Peter credits this experience for his so-called "Sausage Theory." That theory states that we all are pushed through a kind of sausage regarding education, habits, and ways of thinking. But what is the truth, and what is not the truth? It is the challenge of your own life. But to do that, you have to get out of the sausage. Peter says, "You have to leave the comfortable, structured ways of thinking that you have always known and have been doing, to discover what is out there, out of the sausage. You have to respond to what is available and what is needed, not your preordained plans that taught to you, back in your country or your environment." This theory has become a mainstay of his new thinking. Through personal experience in Kinshasa, he discovered it, where he had to adapt intensively to the circumstances, change his way of thinking, and solve things. We have to stop trying to find a Western cure for African malady situations.

Peter experienced the biggest emotional impressions while working in Benin, a small African country, in 2007. Peter was part of a peacekeeping effort and stationed on the airfield with a couple of helicopters. In the poorest of countries where diseases like Cholera were always around the corner, he experienced one of those moments that will forever be in his memories. A woman cleaned their offices a few hours each day and spent the rest of her time selling pineapples to make a living. Peter, who is never reluctant to speak to people, asked her questions about her life and life for those around them to better understand the challenges they faced. Over a few months, he got to know this woman, and one day after careful deliberation, she asked him to take her young boy back to Belgium. Her husband was dead, and she had come here as a refugee from Togo and barely survived. She believed that Peter was a good man and would give her a precious young boy a better life. Her actual words were: "Please take my little son with you to Belgium." "Then he will have a better future because I will not be able to give that to him." He was shocked when he realized that this woman would give the ultimate sacrifice, her child, to a stranger with the hope that the only way she can truly show her love is to give the child away. "It was proof of the love of a mother for her child." I will add to Peter's commentary that I have heard this story from others serving in war-torn regions. My friend Jose Cohello, a Portuguese Air Force Officer, had the same thing happen in Africa.

In Afghanistan 2008, Peter was running the Kabul airfield flying operations for NATO. Peter had an Afghan counterpart who was running the civilian operations. Mr. Sediqi was 70 years old, worked seven days a week, and earned $150 a month. He lost half of his family during the war, and the only thing he could do was keep on working to feed his family. He was a very proud man working hard to survive. He also met a carpet shop owner with sons the same age as Peter's. He asked these young men about their future. These boys went to school from 7 am-2 pm every day and worked in their father's shop in their spare time. They dreamed of a better future, a chance to live in a peaceful land and give their children a better life than theirs. Peter bought some carpets to pay their school fees as the father was very proud and would refuse an outright gift. Peter followed them for a while and still wonders what the future they will have with a country is still very much at war.

It was during his stay in Tampa, Peter and I met. He was working with the fifty-plus nations who had representatives joined in the mission of fighting international terrorism. It became apparent how his assignment as Senior National Representative to Central Command could benefit Peter. He had served in the past in several postings with international officers and soldiers from other nations. 2010. He speaks several languages, his country is in the middle of Europe, a mix of languages, cultures, and habits, and he so fits right in. I will say from knowing many of the officers who served with Peter at that time that they found him very insightful and very contactful. Representing a small nation, he tried to bring a different viewpoint to the table and the meetings. He challenged the business as usual approach to war that never seemed to get to a final solution by posing what he called 'the dummy questions.'

"These are the questions that nobody thinks about in an organization. You start thinking about how the organization believes. It requires an outsider, someone who is not already influenced by how the organization thinks, to ask the right questions.

After Peter's time in Tampa at CENTCOM, he became the Commander of the Search and Rescue base on the North Sea of Belgium from 2011 till 2014. The relationship with the military at MacDill Air Force Base in Tampa with the community was exceptional, and I was an example of that. In Europe, the civilian communities did not always love the military. Maybe they remembered the many wars fought over farmers' land, destroying their crops and homes. Europe has been the scene of many conflicts, and somehow, that feeling is part of the European genes, making them reluctant to make military matters and investments. Peter spent a lot of his time keeping a close relationship with the people of the nearby towns near the base. He instituted some novel ideas. One was using the runway for a competitive marathon and organizing an open door policy so the neighbors could understand the base's mission. It was a difficult time back in Brussels with budget costs, forcing the military to rethink the base's use.

He found out his next career assignment would be at Air Force headquarters in Brussels. The Belgium Air Force had just decided to purchase thirty-four F35 fighter jets from the US. This purchase was a big deal for Belgium. Peter went to Brussels headquarters, explaining a new plan that could integrate the best of everything by reducing the Search and Rescue base and optimizing its functionality. He suggested they purchase fewer planes and add some new NH90 helicopters. Peter was a helicopter pilot and knew they were the most efficient way to do logistical support and humanitarian and disaster relief. Belgium has always been a country that has done a great job on these kinds of missions. Also, these kinds of tasks get a lot of support from the civilian population. He talked to the top Generals and argued that Belgium had a reputation for being one of the best for this kind of work. His arguments could not change their mind. It is the moment for Peter to review his life and make decisions. If what you want to stand for is not aligned with the organization you work for, one has to make a decision. Peter decided to leave the military; he took his retirement and decided to start doing something different. As he said, "I left the military in 2015. I decided to leave sooner than planned. I still think that the military is a useful tool, but we have to do more if we want to have a better world. I am now using my experiences to 'inspire' other people to think "out of the box." He believes that there are other answers, but it demands reflection and the courage to ask the questions, 'why?' and 'Is that the only or best solution?'. For Peter, politics and the media are not telling us the full story of possibilities. We are too easily fooled by not getting the complete information or all the pieces of the puzzle, and we need to stand up to force politicians to think more comprehensively and holistic."

Retirement was not an end for Peter, but a beginning for him to action using what he had learned. He understood that all the people he met in this world, especially the women, want the same things; a safe place for their families, a chance for a better life for themselves and their children, some food, and a roof over their heads. "In my career, I met a lot of people who asked me for help. I realized that education for children might be the key to a better world. So I started helping the people I worked with on my postings. I did not just give them money; no, I wanted to help them giving their children a chance for an education. So mainly, I helped them by paying school fees so that the children could remain in school.

So this all set the stage for Peter's next mission, I will share this in his own words. "Well, in 2009, I decided to go to Kenya on vacation with some friends. All the experiences of my military career attracted me to nature and the people in black Africa.

Kenya has the advantage that it is a relatively safe country that has a lot to offer. Tropical temperatures, beautiful beaches, safari. Most tourists will stay in the hotels and do a safari, but we were renting a big apartment and exploring the environment."

I have a natural tendency to talk to the local people; I ended up with my group in a village where I met John, the local football (Americans call it soccer) team coach. He invited us to a game in the town on Sunday afternoon. The boys were playing barefoot on a field that had six palm trees in the middle. The coaches welcomed us to watch, and the boys played very well. It was a wonderful afternoon. The coaches explained that playing football kept them off the streets and away from getting into criminal activities.

Again we find sports as a way to attract children to change. Wow! Even though all of them were very poor, this gave them a way not to give in to the easy way of survival by stealing and becoming criminals. So it was there, and then I decided to start the project to help these children. I decided to start by helping my friend John's two children to finish primary school.

When I got back to Belgium, I continued to follow them, and the school remained in my thoughts. Then, in 2012, I left for a short vacation to Kenya with my two sons. As young adults, they searched their way through life and struggled with the challenges of how they fit in. I thought this trip to Kenya and meeting the children over there would open their eyes in a good way. I was so right, and they got connected again with themselves and the boys in this small Kenyan school. It ended up being a valuable life lesson for them. And then, something strange happened. Remember the disasters of the Tsunami and the earthquake in Haiti? He tells us, "Many of the people in my country got frustrated because television shows raised a lot of money for these disasters. Two years later, it seemed like a lot of this money was still not spent, was still sitting in banks, or had been spent towards companies who benefit from disasters. People came to me and asked me what I was doing in Kenya. My friends were interested and told me that they would prefer to donate to my project rather than a big organization. I told them they would help children in this school and see how their money made a difference."

So two children became five and then ten, and I began to help more and more children. Finally, in 2014, I created a small board so that more people could get involved and help.

We soon sponsored about 30 children in a primary school, a high school, college, technical schools, and university. During my visit in 2015, I visited another small primary school in the village. Six hundred children were sitting in small classes, without water, electricity, and only four toilets. There we decided that we also could help the school in improving infrastructure. We started with a water tower and a connection to the electricity grid. Step by step, we made improvements. Now, in 2020, about fifteen children finished school with a diploma or a certificate. In Lightmoon Primary Academy, there is water, electricity, a bathroom with sixteen toilets, and we have renovated all the classes. We continue our work. Step by step, we are improving a small part of the world. It is not always massive projects and throwing money at problems. Sometimes it is the little ways we can affect change. "

If you want proof that a long-term policy is working, here is one. In 2020, the Corona virus was challenging the world. Schools and businesses have been closed, and the poor people (again) are suffering the worst.

Here is a message from the school director that Peter has been helping for six years now.

"Dear Mister Peter,

I am so happy and proud for your support in Lightmoon Academy. Sincerely speaking, you have done a lot which has led to our school not being closed down like other schools. The water is paramount during this pandemic times, I couldn't have installed the hand washing stations in the school without the water tower. You have given us a good look, as I flash back from how you found the school years ago. Toilets also are very important now. Our school is very clean now, compared to other small schools like us. The floors in the classrooms and in between te classes, it is all very wonderfull. We can receive the children back, who otherwise should have forced to stay home and remain in poverty.

Many thanks, God bless you all".

Peter Van Den Broucke is one of a kind. An intelligent man sees the world around him clearly and needs to be engaged and not stay silent. His work in Kenya is just the start for him on a road that teaches us important things. Peter is still working in Kenya, and here is how you can help.

Website: www.helpkidstoschool.be
Belgium Account: "HELPKIDSTOSCHOOL"
IBAN: BE16 7340 3515 9374
BIC: KREDBEBB

All financial support goes entirely towards the support of children and the support of schools. None of the gifts will be used for overhead costs or any other personal costs.

If you want to experience a beautiful African country, the beaches, a safari, the people, and the project, contact Peter, and perhaps one day, you can join him on one of his trips.

photo: *Mother who offered up her child to Peter*

photo: *Hem Pun at morning prayer*

chapter 13

HEM PUN AND THE BHARSE VALLEY

I Travel to a Remote Place
with a Man Seeking World Peace

I first met Hem Pun on my first trip to Nepal. He was an uncle of then Major Prem Pun, the Senior National Representative to Central Command, who you might remember introduced Hemu Adhikari to me, which resulted in the starting of Global Action Coalition. He picked me up from my small hotel in Thamel in Khatmandu and took me to a meeting of the local Bharse Community that lived in the city. They gave me an overall of the challenges the community faced and asked if I could help. Hem wanted to take me to Bharse, a small valley community in Gulmi, to see their needs. The people of this region had a long history of supplying military men to Great Britain, India, and Nepal as they were the Ghurkas, the famed fierce fighting force. I met many proud men and women who shared either that they had served or had family members who had, which was a significant honor to the village. It also, at one point, was the primary source of income. With less need for Nepal Ghurkas in foreign militaries, the community was challenged to keep their youth from leaving to the allure of the big cities. They also needed new revenue sources. They had turned to grow different fruits, including cherries and kiwi.

He then traveled to Chitwan to meet me and take me to his remote village. We started from Chitwan after my visit to Uperdang Gadi, which I told you about it in an earlier chapter. We traveled through Butwal to Tansen. In Tansen, we met with another former Senior National Representative to Central Command, Colonel Bharat Gurung, now the local garrison commander. He gave us a tour of this beautiful old city, known as the 'City of the White Lake,' named that because the white clouds come in and the view from above is of a peaceful lake. It has the Kewari Bazaar, a place many come to trade goods. I stayed in what was a new hotel that seemed very modern. The only problem is that the plumbing contractor did not understand that water traps are used on the drain lines to keep the waste fumes from the bathroom. When I went in to shower, I was met with a horrible odor and had to keep the bathroom door closed. My visits to the toilet were quick, and I set a new record for the fastest shower while holding my breath. We left the following day with plans to drive up to Bharse in a Land Rover we rented. We reached a small town by the river at the edge of the Gulmi province, where the road turned off to climb to his village. There we were notified by Hem's friends that the road had been closed because of a landslide. Landslides are a significant threat to the rough roads that are the highways of this country. They travel through mountain passes, and road closures often happen. I promised my next visit we would make it up there. Two years later, on my second trip, we traveled to one of the most beautiful places, this valley where his family had lived for generations. I found this was no ordinary trip since the one road in was like a wide hiking trail with zig zags up into the mountains. Roads in

Nepal have no guard rails, and this one was a humdinger. A one-lane track where you could see the river a thousand feet below just inches from your tires. We traveled up there in a land rover, and when we arrived at this picturesque village perched on the hillside, it was well worth it, though I did have a sigh of relief. The village leaders and elders immediately met us.

I was introduced to each of them; they had been told of my coming and were excited to meet me. One lady asked me if I knew a person from Pittsburg. This man had come to their village 20 years before with the Peace Corp. He had left an indelible mark from his caring and teaching the children. The lady thought America was not that big and I might know this person. When I tell this story around Peace Corp alumni, they all speak of similar stories of the power of goodwill left behind by others who have served in this great organization.

I stayed in a little outbuilding next to his sister's home. I slept on a bench area on some bedding. It was a quiet place, and down the path was the outhouse, and next to his sister's house was a hose fed from a nearby spring that was the water I used to wash with. I was so exhausted that I did not hear the young girls who came to do a ritual dance to welcome me.

This area is quite remote, and there is only solar power for some lights and no internet here. I know Mahabir Pun will make wireless possible here in the future, but it was not at this time.

In Bharse, the central school went from elementary to high school in the village, and in nearby valleys were several small elementary schools. When they graduated, these small elementary schools of about 40 students had their students travel to this middle and high school. We set out to visit the smaller satellite schools accompanied by the Principal of the central school and a teacher who also spoke English. The hike was beautiful, with incredible vistas with views from the ridgeline of Annapurna in the distance, one of Nepal's highest mountains. There was this pathway I saw that led up the mountain to a small religious shrine. I did not have time to climb up there, but I used that photo in the front of the book to give you a sense of the area. After we hiked up to the ridgeline, we had a lot of walking down to get to the small village school. This part of the hike activated an old injury to my knee, which slowed us down.

We did get to visit that one school before I limped back. At this school, I talked with the young students. One asked where I was from, so I asked the teacher if they had a globe or map of the world to show them. They had neither, I was disappointed in not being able to explain how far I had come, and the next time I traveled to Nepal, I carried many blow-up world globes to distribute. The next day we headed to another school still in the other direction from =the central school. We traveled partly by motorcycle and the rest on foot. I was able to hobble up the last bit. We got there early, and while Hem headed off to meet with the elders to plan a small ceremony, I was left sitting outside. A couple of boys were playing with a small soccer ball. It was well worn, and any American family would have thrown it away. The ball came rolling over to me. I sent it back, and soon, much to my delight, we were in the midst of a game. I was showing them no-look and behind-the-back passes, and before long, the numbers of children playing grew until the whole schoolyard was filled with happy, yelling kids. I even got the girls to join in. This experience is still one of the most cherished times in all my trips. Shortly afterward, the village elders began the ceremony of welcoming me.

I had, at this point, achieved nothing, yet they were showing me so much honor. Soon they were putting leis around my neck and painting my face with tika, a red marking. Next, we had a series of speeches in the local Nepali dialect, which Hem translated into English. During the speeches, I pretended to throw an imaginary ball to different kids sitting quietly listening. They immediately got the idea and pretended to catch it and throw it back. Between the honoring by the elders and the fun

I shared with the children, this was a fantastic experience that inspired me. Finally, after many meetings, we ended my three-day visit by signing a memorandum of understanding with the village to start a lunch program.

I had a surreal moment while sitting by my small lodging at the end of the third day. I was preparing my blog of the highlights of the visit. I was also downloading the photos from this trip from my camera into my small laptop. This way, when I got back to Chitwan, I would go to an internet cafe to make calls and send emails. It was at this point, so far away from home, unable to communicate with any of my family, that I experienced a deep wave of homesickness. I felt isolated and alone. All about me, people were speaking in Nepali with the exceptions of Hem and a teacher and the Principal. While working on the photos, Hem's sister, Maya was watching me intently.

Though we couldn't communicate through language as she didn't speak English and I didn't speak Nepali, we still tried to connect. I gathered she wanted to know what I was doing. I thought she would enjoy seeing my wife and my family. Three months earlier, Suzanne and I had been on our honeymoon to New Zealand and Australia, so I realized I could show her Suzanne photos from that trip I had on the computer. I had one of us outside the Sydney Opera House that friends had taken with my camera, and that one must have mystified her. The following image on the computer was of a cruise liner going under the Sydney Bridge. I hadn't thought much about what this must have looked like to Maya. Here was a woman who had never even traveled to Kathmandu trying to fathom what this enormous ship was and going under a bridge over a body of water. She lived in a landlocked nation without any body of water bigger than a river. Later, Hem told me I had shown his sister my magic box. It reminded me of stories of when the Sea Bees were island hopping in the Pacific during World War Two. They would land on a tiny atoll, quickly build an airfield that the Army would use for a few months, and then move on. This was the first contact these native people had with the 'Gods.' Years later, National Geographic did a story on the Cargo Cult, the people who had been forgotten but still worshipped those invaders. The priests wore necklaces adorned with cigarette butts and debris left from the parts of bulldozers and bomber planes.

It was time to leave, and Hem told me they had just started a bus service to this area, and we would take the bus back to Butwal and then on to Chitwan. The trip back to civilization began one of the scariest moments in all my travels. This overloaded bus with the top covered with cargo was not new and started heading down from the mountains. The road was rocky, and the bus was swaying, giving the impression that it could topple over the side to the depths below at any moment. Also, since the road weaved its way down, there was no way the bus could make those sharp turns. So they had sometimes to stop inches from the edge and put it into reverse to back into the hillside so they could turn the bus. Getting into reverse was exciting. As they worked the resisting gears making an awful grinding noise, the bus slid forward closer to the edge, but finally, the gear caught, and we were on our way. At one point, we passed another vehicle on the small road. We were on the outside, and the bus tires were inches from the edge as we slowly wormed our way forward. I kept praying we would make it and remembering that Bhante, the Buddhist monk, once said if he was going to die to keep a smile on your face, so you come back in the next life happy. Hem and I finally reached safety, and much later, I got to an internet café and let Suzanne and my daughter know I was still alive.

Now that you have heard my tale of adventure, it is time to share Hem's story. Hem was the focus of a documentary filmed by the University of Tromso, Norway called Silencing the Guns. It is a compelling visual journey into his life and the life of others who experienced the Maoist War. I will try to share that story with you.

Pun served in the Nepali Army all over the world. The Nepal Army has a history of being used in many peacekeeping roles in conflict areas, and he was an observer in the Republic of Congo and Lebanon. When the Maoist guerrillas fought a war in Nepal from 1996-2006, Hem was a Major in their Army. Hem was wounded in an ambush, and his injury to his leg still bothers him to this day. At some point, the Maoists took the Bharse valley and, realizing they had a family member of a

Nepali officer, took his sister, Maya, hostage. His first thought was he had to go up there and rescue her. Then after thinking it through, he decided that the only result of him bringing the Army there would be to get innocent villagers killed and bring bloodshed to a peaceful valley. It was a hard decision, but one he later realized was the right one. After the war was over and the Maoists were going to be partners in the government of Nepal, Hem realized he felt he could help make the peaceful transition better. So he reached out to many Maoist veterans who were wounded to work with him for peaceful reconciliation. He thought that having a shared experience of being damaged in the fighting could now be a reason to find some common ground. I don't think he ever was successful, but it began a desire to understand more about conflict resolution. Hem Pun, who had been medically retired from the Army, started a search for something different. He was now on the road for peace and reconciliation, community development, and social awareness. He realized this had to start at the grass-root level in remote villages of Nepal as well as the cities. He articulates himself as a peace seeker in upholding the philosophy of Nelson Mandela "Forgive, do not forget." He likes to add one more issue: "know the root causes of conflict of a society." Pun believes in learning by doing, as he has experienced that just a simple action on the field is more meaningful to thousand words or a hundred books on peace. In following his dream, he got a Graduate Certificate in Conflict Transformation Across Cultures at SIT Graduate Institute, World Learning, Vermont, in 2016. That same year he visited with me in the Upstate of South Carolina. He took time out to talk with students and faculty at Clemson University, Furman University, and the University of South Carolina in Spartanburg. His message of peace and reconciliation is one that I hope he continues to promote.

photo: *Hem at the beginning of trek*

photo: *Soledad in Cuba*

chapter 14
SOLEDAD PAGLIUCCA

*Determined to Show
the World a Kindly Face*

With his work in Africa and his service in other 3rd world countries, Peter brought to mind another person. Soledad, or Sole as she is known, who, when I asked to interview her, didn't believe she belongs in this book. I disagreed, so I will leave it to you, the reader, to make your judgment.

Sole talks about her life and the decisions she made along the way, saying, "It was almost like I had no choice, feels good, feels right, so I did it."

Her story starts with her growing up in Palermo in Sicily, Boston, Washington DC, and St Augustine, Florida. She was determined to be different than her mother, who was powerless in her life. She chooses to champion those who were fighting for their fundamental rights and their lives. For later, let us return to her native Italy, where she had become successful in the Italian film industry. She used her talents in language to do the translation of films for dubbing and production. She was often used in minor roles in some of the movies and was successful and in-demand enough that she was able to avoid being sexually harassed by the film executives. She loved her life and lived comfortably in Rome, enjoying the film industry's life, and had many friends. She found love with a man named Peppe McIntire and discovered they shared an adventurous spirit. They decided to make a road trip to India with Peppe's father. This trip ended in tragedy in Pakistan; Pepe's father, who had lost one lung to tuberculosis, collapsed and died suddenly in the middle of the desert. It made them both realize the impermanence of life, so they eventually made their way to the US. Intrigued by Cuba, they decided to visit.

During this time, the Soviets were everywhere on the island, and their influence was still powerful. Many children of that period had names like Vladimir and Alexi. Sole and Pepe loved the island and its people and decided they would like to stay but could not work there. Feeling unnecessary and frustrated, they left, but a seed had been planted. The dormant desire to help others in need had surfaced, and they proceeded to volunteer to work for a human rights organization in Guatemala called Peace Brigades. It was founded in 1981 to protect human rights using non-violent means. It was the only non-governmental organization (NGO) still working there. Their aim in this brutal country was to help women and families whose relatives had disappeared in the many massacres. There were stories of people being locked in churches then set on fire. However, it was a terrible time that did not stop women from protesting and talking about atrocities. They formed a group called "Grupo de Apoyo Mutuo" (Mutual Support Group). The team of volunteers offered their home/office to the group for their meetings, accompanied members to encounters with government officials, and contacted foreign embassies and journalists to publicize their plight. When the indigenous members came into town to share the horrific stories, their home was the "safe" meeting place. Unfortunately, these meetings put the volunteers in danger too. They would also go up to these mountain villages, traveling for hours on old buses, usually alone and at risk, to investigate and report to the UN.

They stayed in the country until forced to leave when two of the leaders of their group were killed.

Sole and Peppe began working in nearby Honduras for the UN High Commission for Refugees. Unfortunately, only one of them was allowed to work in the refugee camps in Honduras as the conditions were awful.

Tragedies and massacres were happening every day, causing a massive influx of Guatemalan and Salvadoran refugees into Honduras. Their next posting was in Nicaragua. Under Daniel Ortega's rule, this country tried to use Cuba as a government model yet learn from its mistakes. For example, in Nicaragua, religion was not frowned upon, and they did not take away private property, yet to the United States, they were a threat as a socialist country.

The US used the Nicaraguan Contras working from Honduras to fight a bloody war to overthrow the Sandinistas. The country was in turmoil and dangerous, especially as they worked at the border where there was always fighting. They met many Cubans working in the medical staff over the eight years they were there and found them to be the loveliest people.

Sole and Peppe founded ProNica, which did humanitarian work throughout the country.

Soledad's work was with the indigenous people, has created a woman's center in Puerto Cabezas. When the women came into the town for health care or better educated, they found a safe place to stay. The women didn't speak Spanish, so one of her projects was to create a dictionary from their native language to Spanish to understand. Nestle had a campaign that the healthiest way to raise their children was by giving bottles of a formula they were selling. This was part of Nestle's war against breastfeeding that helped their bottom dollar.

It was costly and impossible during the war to create the conditions necessary for proper hygiene.

Mother's breast milk had antibodies that would keep the babies healthier, and so they created billboards to educate the mothers. There were always funerals happening in the middle of that war, which emotionally challenged the aid workers. Years later, Sole had dinner with a retired American general and realized that they had been on different sides of that war. She told him that many times while ferrying pregnant women sick with dengue fever from a remote village to Pearl Lagoon across the river, his US-backed Contra troops were firing on them.

Finally, Sole and Pepe succumbed to their dream to travel back to Cuba. They decided to backpack and hitch rides around the whole country. During the fall of the Soviet Union, The Russians were still in Cuba, and it had not yet opened up to tourism. They could not find a way to stay and work, but they could see that help was needed, especially in the more remote areas.

They went back to Florida and came up with the idea of working with an alternative Sister Cities program for Cuba. They participated in a Sister Cities conference in Mobile, Alabama, and then a follow-up conference in Havana. They asked to be paired up with Baracoa, the easternmost city. The people in Baracoa were super excited, and they got a royal carpet welcome. The next step was to engage the city of St. Augustine, where they lived. The response was exactly the opposite. The Cuban community came out in full force and brought in a busload from Miami to the City meeting. The proposal was soundly defeated. Many Cubans are still very angry at the Castro regime after losing their properties when they left. The younger Cubans are more interested in their mother country and getting a chance to visit and meet their lost family members. It turned out to be the best thing ever as they decided with like-minded friends to create an independent friendship association. For the first ten years, they were paired with Institutio Cubano de Amistad con Los Pueblos (ICAP) and were able to work with small groups and towns and in the eastern area, especially Baracoa. Soledad and Pepe never meant for The St. Augustine-Baracoa Friendship Association to be a money-making project. But, it was nourishing both spiritually and emotionally to everyone involved, and that was satisfaction enough. Over the years, they have undertaken incredible projects. An important one was when Hurricane Ike hit the town of Baracoa. They went to Canada with some board members, filled a container, and shipped it out of Nova Scotia. It contained mattresses, clothes, dishes, pots and pans, and other household items, much of which came from donations by local thrift stores. They arranged for the ship to deliver the supplies directly to Moa's eastern port town and then overland to Baracoa. They gave the items to different communities devastated by the hurricane. There was never enough. They also worked with Working Bikes Org. based in Chicago. With their help, the container with 350 bicycles and spare parts and tools went to Baracoa. You can still see those bikes on the streets. Hurricane Sandy was another time they sent a container filled with desperately needed items. In all, they sent 23 forty-foot containers to Cuba. For Hurricane Mathew, they had to bring huge suitcases filled with donated things. There are also scholarships available for university education, specific projects, and attending international conferences. You might be surprised, but I have found the people willing to talk about anything in my visits. Though you will see many billboards for solidarity, I have never felt any sense of people watching me as an American or spying on me. I am not defending Castro's but commenting that not everything you hear is black and white. We always need to question what we are told and learn the nuances behind the news. The people of Cuba are our family, and the work Sole does is all about helping people. Every time I have been there, she is hugged and welcomed as a dear family member, and it is very touching. At some point, her work changed from focused humanitarian work to support artists and writers. She felt that they had enough to eat, but it would be the arts that would address the intellectual and creative needs that, in a small way, could make a big difference. These artists and writers were very talented and deserved recognition, not to become rich but to give them a venue to express themselves. Over the years, she has supported them by bringing in art materials as the artists painted on old sheets and anything they could use. They started bringing in paintbrushes, paints, canvas, and sketchbooks. They built amazing relationships with artists. One of the first books they published was about the Tibaracon group of artists and teachers of Baracoa. The last time I flew in, I carried an electric guitar and amp donated for a young child to use. While in Baracoa, we had a concert with some young students, playing those musical instruments from Sole's previous visits. Other books about the culinary arts and architecture of the area have been printed. The books were free, and the writers and artists could sell them to tourists and make money to continue to support their efforts. An upcoming one is about the region's handicrafts, and it is sure to be a beautiful book.

For Soledad and also Peppe opening the door to Cuba was for them infectious. They became family. They were happy to be a part of this land and, finally, after 35 years, very grateful to be included in that community. So this successful film creator left a good life and helped so many people in many countries. She is an inspiration to me, and I hope to you.

I got to meet Sole when I started showing a Cuban Art collection at Nuance Galleries. She introduced me to some of the artists that were in my collection that I had not met. The artwork was collected by Clyde Hensley, who drove the boat and

dived on the Nuestra Senora de Atocha with famed treasure
hunter Mel Fisher. It had become the focus of an exhibition that
traveled to museums and universities for four years, reaching
fourteen cities and tens of thousands of visitors. Somehow this
art is so fresh and vital that it excited me, which began my love
affair with Cuba. The topping on the cake was when I started
visiting and seeing how tough life was, that they were happy and
so talented. The Friendship Association continues the work of
assisting artists and writers and could always use support. Sole

photo: *Sole with Director of the Institure of Geology and Minerals*

takes people to Cuba and especially Oriente, the easternmost part of the island. She also does birding tours to the western part of Cuba.

Ediciones Nuevos Mundos, the publishing wing of The Friendship Association, has published 25 books written by Cubans for Cubans.

Three more books will be off the press before Christmas. Most of the books, including the book The Painters' Magic (La Magia de sus Pintores), which tells stories of Baracoa's fantastic artists and the region's history, is still available from their website.

The St. Augustine-Baracoa Friendship Association
www.staugustine-baracoa.org

chapter 15

HEIDI KUHN

*From Mines
To Vines*

So how do people find these alternative paths? Heidi found out making a vow; a prayer can open a gate that will transform her life and her entire family.

Sometimes it takes just one or two words to know you have meant somebody important. In this case, Heidi Kuhn cannot talk about her life without referring to her Defining Moments. And for me, that was a signal that I had to get to know her story. I know you will see it is a good one.

Heidi comes from a pioneer and seafaring family. The Maine sea captains were originally Scottish Settlers, and for her, that 'no fear can do' family history is an essential part of her character. Her family ending up in California is due to Captain John McNear wanting to be part of the Gold Rush in California in 1856. As luck would have it, he missed connecting to the boat in Panama and had to catch another ship to arrive in California.

This boat sank, and that would have ended the story right there. I think the phrase "Don't curse the darkness light a candle" that Heidi believes shows how this is a family tradition.

So undeterred by any setbacks, McNear arrived and before long started a shipping industry and a bank that bought real estate. They were not the robber barons but found their niche working with everyone, including the Chinese who came seeking a new life. The Chinese were often preyed upon and looked down on, yet they were the work engines that helped create the prosperity of that time.

Respect for the land respect for the people was her family's values.

I share this family history so we can better understand where Heidi's adventurous spirit came from. We start her story with her embarking on a scary opportunity when she traveled to the other end of the world to be an exchange student in Japan. The Vietnam War had ended two months prior, and she was a Rotary Club's youth ambassador to Japan. The date is 1975, and 30 years earlier, the US and Japan had fought a devastating war. For Heidi's parents letting her travel, there was a quantum leap of faith. We are long before cell phones, and the internet and long-distance travel for a young girl seemed dangerous. She remembers being jet-lagged when she arrived at the host family house and idly looking through a family album. One picture that stood out was the father in uniform, standing in front of the Japanese flag. She realized that World War 2 was not that far away, and it came crashing down to her.

At that moment, the father walked in and found her looking at this picture. This meeting could have gone many different ways, but it became a moment of forgiveness and healing in friendship's true spirit. Sitting with this former enemy and realizing that it did not matter, and at this moment, they were friends became one of Heidi's 'defining moments. Heidi came home and told her parents she was going to get an education for peace. She graduated from the University of California, Berkeley, with a degree in Political Economics for industrial Societies. It was an exciting time for Heidi to attend school at the Peace Movement's center against the Vietnam war. She not only began an incredible journey; she also met her husband to be Gary, who became an integral part of her path.

Heidi's next major event happened at age thirty in the form of a diagnosis of malignant cervical cancer. It was 1988, and she had gone to a doctor in Juneau, Alaska, where her husband was the manager of IBM for the state.

Working as the weather anchor for the local CBS affiliate, she had a bad neck ache. The nurse made her go through a complete physical. That nurse somehow intuitively knew that this was something more significant. Since there was no gynecologist in the State of Alaska, they sent the results to a lab in Seattle. The results were alarming, and her doctor in San Francisco received them. She remembers that June day getting a call from her doctor. He starts with Mrs. Kuhn, are you sitting down, and following with you have malignant cancer, and you need to get on a plane right now and get to the hospital here for immediate operation. At first, she couldn't speak, but then she said I can't go to San Francisco right now; I have three little kids. He said, get on the next plane, or you will never have a chance to see them grow up. The diagnosis was so severe that before the operation, they gave her last rites. Waking up from the surgery on the 4th of July, she could see outside her hospital window; the sky was alight with fireworks. Heidi was blessed, and the operation was a success and went back to Alaska with a chance to see things through a new lens. Before going under the knife, she prayed to God. "Dear God, grant me the gift of life, and I will do something with it". Another of her 'defining moments' had happened, and Heidi would soon find out what that prayer was going to bring forth. Now it is 1995, and she is back with her doctor. Again he comes in with a grave face. She says whatever you have to say, say it fast. His response blows her mind.

The words you are pregnant come out when you expect to hear you are going to die. Fast forward two years, and in 1997, the world saw the amazing Princess Diana walking through the minefields of Angola. This miracle child was born after an operation that she believed had ended any possibility of that ever happening. Heidi brought home with her a beautiful infant named Christian. The plight of people living in the remnants of war-torn countries moved her, and nine months later, she walked the minefields of another devastated country, Bosnia Herzegovina. Diana died three weeks later, and this loss crushed the world. However, her incredible acts of bravery and compassion inspired many to action.

Heidi now had her own news company and became known throughout California as a caring person. She got a call from the Commonwealth Club of San Francisco, a think tank hosting a speaker on landmines. They wanted to use her house for a fundraiser. Heidi now had four children; she was wondering if she could pull off this event. She decided to do it and was able to get 100 people to her home that evening. She called Francis Coppola to donate some of his wine and invited her friends; some were also vintners from the local area. The room was full of people with good food and wine learning about this poignant subject. Heidi raised her glass and made this toast, "may the world go from mines to vines" This was what Heidi called a 'Catalytic moment.' One of her guests broke the silence and said, "do you realize what you said?" "You now have to take that out of the living room to action." Right there and then, a simple toast became a call for action. Heidi does nothing in a small way. Kofi Annan, Assistant Secretary-General of the United Nations, was at Her launch of the Roots for Peace organization. Also in attendance was a young congresswoman Nancy Pelosi.

Her initial fundraising in the year 2000 was $30,000 with the help of Robert Mondavi, Francis Coppola, other Napa Valley vintners, plus other friends. This amount was matched by the US Department of State Office of Political-Military Affairs Weapons Removal and Abatement. It shows how somebody who has credibility can access their integrity to make things happen.

Her first trip was to Croatia after the Balkan wars, and there were over one million unexploded landmines throughout the country.

She caught the interest of Croatian-born vintner Mijenko Grgich who was strongly motivated to help his native-born country. He helped raise another $250,000 for this project, which was the first step in the Minefields to Vineyards project. They took on demining the area around schools and soccer fields in one of the war-torn regions. Imagine a child could not chase a butterfly across a field or kick a soccer ball out of bounds without losing a limb. Later she traveled there with her daughter. Kyleigh was your typical thirteen years old girl more concerned with designer jeans and boys. She and Mom were taking a trip to Europe, and Heidi asked if it would be ok to stop in Croatia to see what was happening there. If you have ever been to a war zone or a 3rd world country, it is life-changing, and for Kyleigh, this was no exception. Kyleigh saw children tethered to poles like animals while the mothers were working in the fields nearby. This sight seemed inhumane and something you would do to your pets or livestock. Kyleigh asked them why are they tied up? The answer was startling," The parent said the entire backyard is riddled with mines, and if we don't tether the children, they will be tempted to retrieve the only family ball when we are not looking" The parents did not want them to stray into landmines. We worry about our children playing in the streets or someone bullying them. In Croatia, they worry about them getting blown up. For Heidi and her daughter, this was a 'defining moment.' In 2004 a few years later, Kyleigh and Heidi revisited this same village and found the same children playing without restriction in a garden filled with colorful flowers. They sat in the kitchen and had some freshly baked bread and put delicious jam from the berries in that same demined yard.

A few years go by, Kyleigh is now sixteen, and she meets Cheryl Jennings, the ABC news anchor and one of Heidi's friends who was just back from Kosovo. Kyleigh tells her how affected she was by what she saw on that detour of her first trip to Europe and her second time to Croatia and that she wanted to do something to help children facing landmines. Cheryl then asked her what do you want to do? They decided there was a project to demine Afghanistan areas and a desperate need for schools for girls there. So Kyleigh began a penny campaign in high school, and her sharing of her experiences was very motivating. They raised 50 million pennies, which is $500,000, and even Colin Powell contributed and gave his support. It took several armored cars to carry the pennies to the bank.

Going to Afghanistan was a big challenge for the organization. First, they were looking into working in another country, and that was a challenge. This organization, working in the basement of their house. The second challenge was working in a country where there was still a war going on, adding a dangerous element. What changed it for Heidi was learning that Afghanistan had been known for its grapes at one time. Now there were none but the rootstock for those grapes which still existed in California. I think this idea of restoring the ancient vines touched Heidi. The grapes in this country have never fermented grapes as Muslims traditionally do not drink alcohol. The grapes were for the table and for making raisins. Roots for Peace was doing all this work and had a budget of hundreds of thousands of dollars, and they needed to get this small operation out of the basement and get a real office. This boggled my mind. They were doing all this work in two countries with basically no employees and no staff. They had inspired so many people to travel and help raise money.

Angola became the next stop for the Heidi train to impact. She says she was following in Princess Diana's footsteps as this was the place she had first brought the horrific truth to the world in 1997. And now, in 2005, this country still was the most heavily mined place in the world. Unfortunately, it was also one of the most fertile, and so many acres were going to waste.

One tale they heard that stood out was about an Angolan woman eight months pregnant and hungry. She dared to go to some mango trees to pick the fruit. She made it to the tree, and while picking a mango, the landmine went off. She ended giving birth while having her leg amputated. Using money from the penny campaign, they started a major fundraising campaign to match that money.

One of the projects was to build a soccer field on land newly demined. Later, when they went back, one of the boys joked, "now we play on three legs instead of two, one good leg and two crutches. It is amazing how they can joke about their misfortunes.

They also found that elephants were victims of landmines, and the scientists were studying migration patterns to keep them from straying into the minefields.

Cuando Cubango was one place they went as it was one of the more heavily mined areas. On the plane's landing, the pilot told them how important it was to be precise, and they looked out the window and saw landmines protruding from the ground all alongside the runway. Unfortunately, their meeting with two government officials ended up canceled. The men died when their Landrover swerved to avoid a wild animal and hit an anti-tank mine. Heidi wondered if their government officials were not safe, then who was. As I have talked with her and read some of her accounts, I am shocked at how many times she has in this quest to help people far from her California home have been in danger, whether from landmines or killer bees. Through these stories, I learned, every trip she took, she worked with local families, local officials, and the countries' government leaders, plus many Non-Governmental Organizations (NGOs), the UN, USAID, and business leaders winegrowers. They were a coalition inspired by her efforts to promote and support this world project.

On one of her return trips to Afghanistan with her daughter, Kyleigh, who was now in college, was accompanied by ABC news anchor Cheryl Jenkins. The 3 of them arrived at a village whose efforts had enabled the farmers to have a great harvest of grapes where there once were mines. They prayed with the farmers who, in their language, recited verses that said they all served the same God, and all are daughters of Abraham. This is an example of how good works and peace can transform the differences of culture and religion.

Kyleigh noticed a group of children sitting on the ground in the hot sun. She went over to investigate and found them

looking at a chalkboard and realized this was the school. It left
a deep impression on her, and as their trip was winding down,
looking at Cheryl and Heidi, and announced they were going to
build a school for these children on the former minefield across
the road. Kayleigh was much like her mother, and once she gets
an idea in her head, it will be a certainty. So they cleared the
landmines, and the money raised by Kyleigh paid for the school.
The local people named it the Kyleigh Kuhn school. Heidi
was so proud, realizing that building this organization had not
come at the cost of raising her family. Instead, it had become
a shared love that included all of them. They also, on this trip,

met Fawad Afa. He had been a soccer team leader in a game, and when the ball went into the minefield, he felt it his job to retrieve it. Now years later, he had grown up minus that leg. He happened to be the same age as Kyleigh, and they made an instant connection. As they were leaving, Kyleigh told her mom, we can't just go; we have to help him. They found out that of his deep love for soccer, he became their first Afghani employee and the soccer coach for the official Roots of Peace Soccer team. The girl's team became well known as this young man had found his calling. He even took them to compete in Italy at a soccer competition. Later he was working for the Arsenal team in England.

Vietnam is a country where certain areas like near where the DMZwere riddled with land mines, so of course, Roots for Peace decided to go there. Since her days at Berkely, she felt that we had done many wrongs there, and it would be healing to help.

She did not seem to be able to find anyone who would help fund this next step. Finally, she was at a conference and met Heidi, and she asked what she did. Heidi explained her projects, and this woman asked if this program could be replicated anywhere?. Of course, said Heidi, so she took her card. A few days later, she got a call from Tory Dietel Hopps, who wanted to discuss your program in Vietnam. Her husband Gary got on the line too, and they asked how they could help her. She said, "I would like to help you in your work in Vietnam and ended up funding the program in Quang Tri province to the tune of $450,000. I love what Heidi says next in her book. "And People wonder why I pray on Muslim, Buddhist, and Catholic beads."

Before our first trip to Vietnam, Heidi's son Tucker graduated from the University of San Francisco. He asked if he could submit his resume to work for Roots for Peace. Heidi remembered all the dangers almost she had, so she was reluctant. However, her husband, Gary, persuaded her that Tucker was obsessed with their work. He would make a great member of the team and possibly the future of the organization. He quickly became a knowledgeable student of agricultural practices. While in Vietnam, looking at cashews as something to plant suggested they also plant cacao trees between the rows. This newer science of biodiversity with intercropping would expand income and help the soil. It became a huge success.

To date, Roots of Peace has impacted over 1 million farmers and families, spanning eight countries – Afghanistan, Angola, Bosnia-Herzegovina, Cambodia, Croatia, Iraq, Israel, Palestine, and Vietnam. In addition, Heidi's work has led to the successful USAID program in Vietnam.

Some of Heidi's story is from our interview. Some of the other stories are from her book Breaking Ground. This book is an easy read, but there are so many amazing stories, and I hope you are inspired to get the book and share it. I guarantee you will be enchanted.

You can also be part of the Roots for Peace family and support their work in the world. For more information, go to .https://rootsofpeace.org/our-team

every where

p peace always an

photo: *Daniel with one of the 'garbage children'*

chapter 16
DANIEL TILLIAS

I Can Fly and
Here is Why

It is not always people who are so blessed as Heidi or Ramjee, or their work in the military pushes them to help others. None of them had ever known what it was like to live in poverty. Here is a story about someone who had a different path to greatness.

When someone writes a book titled 'I Can Fly' he either is a pilot or has a great message. Well, Daniel fits into the second category. Daniel was nominated as a CNN Hero and was visiting the Upstate of South Carolina recently. Upstate International, of which I am on the Board, invited him to speak, and I thought it would be interesting. Since I have been working in 3rd world countries, I knew I would understand the issues he was facing in his home country of Haiti. What I found was Haiti is a unique experience. I was stunned at his inspirational story and the work he does. Now I will share his story to know why Daniel was nominated for this significant award.

According to Daniel, his success story starts with his Mom. His father died when he was 13, and his mother was trying to raise three sons in a poverty-stricken area of Haiti. She was determined to raise herself and the boys out of the slums of Port Au Prince and live safer and healthier lives. She knew education was the key, and she gave up her happiness to work long hours and pushed them hard to strive for something different. She succeeded in this endeavor, with one son being an Orchestra Conductor and the other working for the US Embassy in Tanzania. Daniel pursued a law career. Part of his study was a requirement to do some community work, and he ended up helping in the prisons giving law advice to men who were gang members dealing with drugs or violence. Daniel realized they had become involved on the wrong side of the law because many felt they had no real choices. His inner voice said that the real work he needed to do was helping his community's youth before they got to jail, giving them opportunities and hope. In 2012, this moment was the actual birth of Sakala; Tillias was instrumental in founding and his Defining Moment in his life. Let's learn through his work what made quitting his law career create this youth empowerment program called SAKALA, which translates to the Community Center for Peaceful Alternatives. So his Mom got him out of the ghetto, and he chooses to dive back in.

We are talking about Cite' Soleil, the garbage dump of Port Au Prince. This place was the largest underserved community in all the country. It's a small location that is densely populated, and yet it is the largest ghetto or the largest slum. Next to the water, surrounded and crossed by several sewers, often clogged because of the poor management of waste. Cité Soleil is often flooded continuously, and it becomes invaded by all the garbage and trash floating through the streets. It has infected the minds of the people. They have evolved to become the refuse themselves.

To make a change seemed an overwhelming task, but Daniel realized that he needed to start with sports to get children involved. Football, or what we know as Soccer in the United States, is Haiti's most popular sport.

Daniel tells of one of the most formidable gang leaders who wanted to talk to him. Daniel went with trepidation, not knowing if he was going to shut me down? Or was he expecting me to pay money to him? It turns out this dangerous man wanted a favor from Daniel. He said I want you to take my brother into your programs; I don't want him to turn out like me! This gang leader on his side was a significant step forward; he could now do his work free from gang interference and reach out to the community's entire youth.

What is also very powerful is that many broken neighborhood parents felt that their children were worthless. So they were forced into gangs or struggled in abject poverty. How could they ever turn out to be different from the garbage dumped there?

Once he had children playing soccer together, he realized he had to start educating them and giving them opportunities. One brilliant idea was to have them scrounge through the garbage to find ways to create art and frames from the waste. Think about it, the transformation of both children and trash into art, or in this case, artists. If you go to Haiti and visit SAKALA, you will find it a haven from outside violence. Near the sports field where children play soccer and basketball, there are classrooms, a library, and a community garden where herbs bloom from old tires once burned in the streets. Now the Largest garden in the country

Daniel said, "kids in Cité Soleil have gone through so much in terms of what they see in the street (or) what they hear all the time. Sometimes it's a natural disaster; then, there will be a flood. They lose nights without sleeping. Our sports are for creating a sense of collaboration. It's sports to build yourself, to understand that you have the potential to reach a goal. It's sports to that develop self-esteem." It is not only sports like soccer, volleyball, baseball, basketball, American flag football, street hockey, and ping pong. We've done a lot of yoga, meditation, and (we've) introduced Tai Chi so they can kind of find a discipline that can focus them as they deal with the challenges they face. One child kept passing by and watching the children playing or studying. Finally, he walked through the gate. It was life-changing. He became fascinated with chess and soon learned the rules and became the local chess champion. He used to torture Daniel when they played. Daniel was frustrated that he could not win against him but was also glad. He has become one of Haiti's chess prodigies.

One of his initiatives Tillias launched was to launch a green initiative to replicate the community garden across the whole island of Haiti. This way, all Haitians can grow their own food. And he hopes the example of the children of SAKALA, who are growing food and promoting peace, will be the ones to pull their families and the entire country from poverty. "We could have a new country that becomes the model for the world. And we know that it can start here," he said.

Daniel now says, "I am so lucky, I think so too, and if you want to support him in this crusade to transform Haiti by helping SAKALA, here is how you can. Watch this video to see for yourself

CNN heroes Creating an oasis of hope in one of Haiti's most dangerous neighborhoods - CNN

OR got to the website to donate, Sakala (sakala-haiti.org)

photo: *Elder from Garabtisan*

chapter 17
ADVENTURES IN DJIBOUTI

You read about my involvement in forming Global Action Coalition and also my first trip to Nepal. I hope this sets the stage for what comes next. Going back to that Thanksgiving day dinner that was one of the origins of this story, you might remember another guest who plays into this story. Colonel Samuel Alito, the Senior National Representative from Kenya, and his son were also present. During the dinner, I had a very informative talk with the Colonel. I wanted to learn more about Africa's issues, and here was a chance to get some insights. He said it was going to be two major challenges facing Africa, education, and water. I think this was another moment that opened a door. Fast forward a few years, and we had already started Global Action, and I had been to Nepal three times with many education projects when I met this amazing man at the St. Petersburg Saturday Market. I was there showcasing the work we were doing at a booth that the Market gives non-profits to showcase what they do. I had set up photos of our food lunch programs and other educational works and enjoyed sharing stories with those interested. Along came this man, who was an inventor working on solar-powered water pumps. I was immediately enthralled. As a young man in my 20s had a brief stint as a plumber and had managed spring-fed water to homes in Tennessee. I decided to meet with this inventor and see his pumps in action, and it spurred me to investigate what else the technology was available at that time. I kept thinking about what Samuel Alito said, education and water, and I thought this could be an important new GAC project. A few weeks later, I was on one of my monthly visits to Coalition Village at CENTCOM, where the 50 plus nations had their offices and the place that Bhante had met the Bangladeshi officers. In those days before the infamous Jill Kelly affair that brought down, the CIA Director retired General Petraeus. To refresh your memory, Jill Kelly was the wife of an Oncologist who had treated the General. She used her connections to put on parties for the Coalition and other senior leaders at Central Command. She went even further, using her influence to try to do some deals, one with the South Koreans. Petraeus, at that time, had been working on his biography with a retired Army Counter Intelligence woman, Paula Broadwell. I won't condemn the General or his biographer for being enticed into an affair. I am sure the intimacy of writing a book with a pretty woman who also understood the world he lived in became a tough challenge to stay platonic. That is their issue to live with, but what made it all crazy is when Broadwell felt threatened to see the communications between the General and Jill Kelly. Mistaking her for being a rival, she called Kelly, and it scared her, and she reported the call to the FBI. This call opened a pandora's box at Central Command, and the repercussions of that affair shut down the base from most community interactions which hurt everyone. Up to that time, I had free reign to visit my Coalition friends, and I would often spend a morning there, starting with the Coffee Working Group and then some drop-ins into offices of the Senior National Representatives of different countries. This was how I could meet with them and find out what I could do to help them. I also worked with the Tampa Bay Lightning and their star defenseman Victor Hedman to get tickets to hockey games for these many countries' visitors. Hedman would give me a suite and ask me to fill it with the international officers and their families, and then after the game, we would head down to the locker room for signed jerseys from him. For such a tough defenseman, he is a sweet and easy-going man. His gift to the officers was always an appreciated evening. I had become connected with the Coalition, these international military officers, in 2002 when the Coalition Coordination Center General Chip Diehl invited me to meet them. Chip had been the Wing Commander at MacDill, and we became friends working together to help the South Tampa community outside the gates of the base and the men and women who came to serve the 6th Air Refueling Wing. So his introduction to the international community serving was the beginning of my understanding of issues more globally. I watched many World Soccer matches with friends who were rooting for their teams. When the last Africa team got knocked out of the Worlds, all of Africa went into mourning. When the US team lost, it was on to football or baseball or….. Whether it was sports or how they viewed the world, it was different and sometimes eye-opening. Another Defining Moment. So I knew many of the officers and had built great friendships. Sometimes I would find problems they were having and was able to offer assistance. This particular morning I wandered into the Djibouti office, and my friend Colonel Mohamed Farah was cooking some traditional Djiboutian food on a hot plate. He offered me a taste, and then we chatted. I asked him what the issues his country faced were?

He said water. One of his country's assets is sunshine, and I later
found out the wind is also a constant. WHAM. So we began
investigating how Solar Powered pumps would work there. He
was finishing his tour of duty and headed back to his country
and invited me to visit him there. It took a few months, and then
I booked a trip to arrive during January as summers in Djibouti
are brutal. Meanwhile, I had done my research into the various
pumps and equipment that were needed. He met me at the
airport, got me settled in a small, inexpensive hotel, and then we
started traveling around his country. Djibouti city is the capital
of Djibouti, and this country is mostly very arid. We had a
driver, and everywhere we went, military and police saluted the
car. I noticed it had an A on it, and I realized it was like an
Ambassador's car. I felt like a visiting dignity. Each day for a
week, we would start from my hotel and then look for water
projects and, since I was doing education projects in Nepal, we
visited the local schools. While visiting a school near the Somali

border, I learned an important lesson. This particular school had been wired for solar power, but it was not working, and nobody knew how to fix it. I vowed in my work never to start something and then leave it to become wasted. On this same trip, I had the most strange experience. We visited the small town of Ali Sabieh, and my friend Mohamed introduced me to the local Colonel from the Djibouti Army. In this small country, they have designated officers to be responsible for areas of the country. There is terrorist activity from El Shabab, a terrorist group there, and a few years earlier, they had blown up a French restaurant in Djibouti city. Besides being on the lookout for terrorists, these officers are also responsible for overseeing the welfare of the area. Everywhere we traveled, we met them, and the locals loved them as they worked to help whenever possible. So Mohamad and this officer took me to a school that needed help. The area had both an influx of Somali refugees and many nomadic people who spent time there. As we were walking up to it, they mentioned a Catholic Priest ran it. I stopped and explained to my hosts that Global Action would not support a school that converted children, and our mission was to respect all religions. They both laughed and said that was not the case and I had to meet Father Jean. I then realized the absurdity of the moment. Here I was, a Jewish man who studied Buddhism and explained to my Muslim friends that we could not support a Catholic Priest. I guess you could say we represented a smorgasbord of the world's religions. Meeting Father Jean was a real treat. He was as down-to-earth as you can be and his dedication to the children was very strong. He had no mission of conversion, just a dedication to help these children. It was at the time of the new Pope Francis, so I asked him his thoughts. I remember vividly his response, "finally a Pope who understands what we are doing."

The water project that was my initial reason for traveling to Djibouti never happened as I could never find the funding, and then I also had to focus on my business. However, what did happen was the opening of another door to continue in a different direction.

Towards the end of our trip, Mohamed took me into the area above the famous Lake Assal. The most beautiful place in Djibouti. It is a salt lake that runs into the Ghoubbel El Kharab bay and then into the Gulf of Tadjoura and the Gulf of Aden. Across the water about twenty miles is Yemen. You see an abandoned salt mine on the road, and from this area, people will gather the salt and carry it by camel northwest into Ethiopia and sell it there. I met several of these men with their camels and thought, what a hard life. In another place, we saw goats in the trees as that was the only green they could eat in this dry land.

We traveled up onto the plateau over a rough road, unable to go faster than five mph, never missing any of the bumps and holes that consisted of this road. Finally, we could see the small village in the distance. We found ourselves on a barren plateau that was the home to the Afar village of Garabtisan, and waiting for us were the women who had gathered to welcome us with song and dance. The only visible features were the small mountains on either side and a large watering hole. Across the water, camels were standing in the water while drinking it. I asked if this the drinking water for the village?. The Army Colonel assigned to this area said yes and took a cup and went down to the water and filled it up and drank from it.

My first thought was if I did that, I would not survive the night. The village's only structures were small yurts, a type of hut scattered around, a small building used to store food from the World Food Bank, and a tattered UNICEF tent. The elders of the village had assembled in the tent to meet me. The people there spoke the Afar language, which then was translated into Somali, which Mohamed translated into English. The elders explained that this one tent was all that was usable for their school. The other tents had been ripped or blown away by the wind, and I could tell this one was also not in great shape. I told them I would help them get their children back to school. I felt this was something that I had to do. The response was, "are you just saying that, or will you be back to help fulfill your promise." This comment went right through me like a spear. It makes me wonder how many times Aid organizations had promised to do something and never returned, not only here but also worldwide. Nevertheless, I was determined to follow through. I felt this elder's plea was for their children and was a call for action. I went back to my hotel, deep in thought.

I had met many people here, from nomads by the roads' side to villagers in these remote areas that I was not sure how they survived, but those up in this wasteland were proud that they owned their land. On our last drive, our driver asked if he could stop and pray as the call for prayer was sounding as we drove through the town of Arta. While we waited, a group of boys came over to our land rover. One was wearing a shirt with the name of Messi, and I teased him and said Ronaldo, he replied Messi, and before long, I was involved in a game of soccer using an empty soda can. It is moments like these that show we are all alike, and the key to that global understanding can be as simple as a faux soccer ball. I vowed that the next time I came, I would bring soccer balls and leave some in this village. In my time in this strange yet fascinating country, I have much gratitude to Mohamed Farah for his hospitality, support, and his genuine caring about the people of his land.

I returned to my home in Tampa, a man on a mission. I figured with all the used tents in Afghanistan and Iraq not needed anymore, I could easily find some used tents to send back to Djibouti. I used every contact I had at CENTCOM, SOCOM, SOCCENT to no avail. I also contacted the J4 (logistics), Deputy Commander, at AFRICOM (African Command). I had better step back and explain as the military world is full of acronyms. Stationed at MacDill Air Force

Base are two of the major commands of the world. Central Command (CENTCOM) oversees our military interests in the Mideast and has been fighting the war on terrorism. You will remember some of the Generals from there, Petraeus, Mattis, and now Secretary of Defense Lloyd Austin. In my helping the American and international serving there, I had gotten to know all of them. Special Operations Command (SOCOM) is the Navy Seals, Green Berets, and other highly trained military from the other branches. Special Operations Central Command (SOCCENT) is a smaller unit that works between the two larger ones. African Command based in Europe, and Djibouti is part of their Area of Operation (AOR). Djibouti is also involved with CENTCOM as the Horn Of Africa is the base dealing with Somalian piracy and nearby Iran. I had developed some friends among these commands but still no tents.

I remember going to the German National Day celebration, and that year, it was in a building downtown Tampa. I was looking for Dennis D'Angelo, the J4 Deputy at Centcom, and I ended up meeting his boss, Major General Ed Dorman. He asked what I was up to, and I explained our search for tents to put children back to school in Djibouti. His response was, "I can get you some tents." After a year and a half of knocking on doors and many long-distance chats, I had found the tents. I was blown away, almost like those tents in the village. The tents were Blue Med Shelters owned by Alaska Structures and were in a warehouse in Dubai. He then asked how I was going to get them to Djibouti. I had not planned that far ahead. He had an answer for that, and he could get President Shipping Lines, now known as APL ship them there for free. I remember his organizing a phone call with people in Idaho and Dubai, plus some in other parts of this country, to discuss the logistics of moving the tents. The funny part was I was there representing the Djibouti Army, my partner in this venture. The next thing and the tents were on their way. Now I had to get myself there too.

photo: *My dear friend Mohamad Farah at Garabtisan*

photo: *Rob with Grand Douda leader and Djibouti Army soldiers looking on*

chapter 18

DJIBOUTI, I RETURN TO FULFILL MY PROMISE AND LEARN ABOUT MYSELF

We begin this story with me back home in Tampa Bay. Somewhere on the sea, the tents traveled on a long route from Dubai to Indonesia and then back to the Mideast to Djibouti. Free is free, and I was so thankful for American President Lines for their generosity in bringing the tents to Djibouti. I had decided to be in Djibouti to meet the ship, believing I might have to be there if we had trouble getting the tents off the ship. My partners, the Djibouti Army, were going to pick them up. Little did I know that even with the Army involved, we would still have someone trying to hold us up for bribes.

At this time, a young lady, Elana, wanted to help Global Action Coalition's work. When we talked, I told her about this project, and she asked if she could come. Elana was excited about the idea of being an intern with us and learning in the field, or in this case, the desert. She said she would pay her own way, so I said ok after discussing this with the GAC Board. As I had said, the plan was to meet the ship when it arrived, and this was a mistake on my part. We had also arranged to have a couple of men from Alaska Shelters there, and I had raised money to pay for them. The installers stayed at the USAID team leader's home, who had volunteered to help in any way he could. The reason I felt these men were necessary were the tents were not your ordinary pup tents but were complicated structures, and it took training to assemble. So we arrived, and not long after, the men who were to build them and the tents were stuck on the dock. We were staying at the same hotel I had stayed in the last time. This was not one of the name hotels that started at $250 a night close by; these rooms cost was $80 a night and were affordable for our travel budget. The rooms were simple, with a weak shower fed by a tank on the roof. Luckily there were no mosquitos in the rooms, though they had left the windows open sometimes. I always made sure not to leave the door open when going in and out and the window shut. The air conditioning unit was overhead, and keeping the right temperature was always a challenge.

The breakfast room was open to outside, and it required you to pay attention to mosquitoes while eating your breakfast. I would see them in the lobby, even with the fans going on. Considering how dry Djibouti is, the mosquitos thrive here. I will continue to set the scene. In Djibouti, like Nepal, I was on guard for my health. You cannot drink the water from the tap or let it in your mouth during showering or forget and brush your teeth with it. Ice in your water is also a no-no. I also bring a blow-up pad under the sheets to make the hard bed a little more bearable.

I had one of my darkest nights. I was still jet-lagged, lying in my hotel room. I am sure everyone has had one of those nights. My mind kept spinning, envisioning all the worst possibilities, and I wondered if I have put my intern in danger. Perhaps she could get bitten by a mosquito or eat or drink something that gets her sick. It is one thing worrying about myself, but this was the first time I had someone else to think about. I was also concerned that we could get the tents off the dock and not lose too many days. Without the tents, they cannot help get them up.

I have always believed that worrying is useless. Wayne Dyer once said that if you have a problem, then if you can do something about it, do it and then let it go. If you cannot do anything, then let go. Worry does not affect the outcome except in making you less able to be sharp and present. From about age 50, my father was scared he would get cancer and die as his father had. He did lose his life to cancer at age 89. In the time between, he lost many years of his life in worry, I vowed not to do the same. Yet here I was in this foreign room, lost in fear of failure or health issues.

The following day knowing that I would be losing my assembling team soon, I realized I needed another expert source to help. Djibouti is the home of many military bases. Besides the US military, there are French, Italian, Japanese, Saudi Arabia, and even Chinese contingents. The US base Camp Lemonier is the home for the Horn of Africa headquarters; one of its mission is to watch over piracy from Somalia. I found out the base had a US Navy Sea Bee group. I called the Naval Commander there. Yes, he said there was a SeaBee battalion there, but their policy said they could not help an NGO (non-governmental organization). I explained how we would be helping the country, and I was not making money off of this. He seemed unmoved. I then went to try a different tack. I shared with him that I had been a board member of the US Navy League. I had helped commission a couple of Aegis class destroyers (Lassen and Bulkeley). Finally, I had a retired Rear Admiral who had been Deputy Commander of CENTCOM on my Advisory Board. He started to realize I was a friend to the US Navy, and I heard his tone change. His following words thrilled me. "I cannot help you, but I can do a training exercise with the Djibouti Army," So I ended up having the support of the SeaBees and even their bulldozer to help level the site near the base in the town of Douda. I remember as a child reading a Landmark Book about the Seabees in WWII. They were essential in our march across the Pacific Ocean, building airfields on tiny atolls to project our air power. Often they were under fire and never got recognition for their efforts. So now I had these fantastic sailors to help teach and erect these tents. Djibouti Army Chief of Staff of the Djibouti Army had

photo: *SeeBees, and Alaska Shelters, Djibouti Army finish ADPEB school tent*

to get involved in releasing them, and we lost a couple of days of valuable time. However, now we still had the installers from Alaska Shelters, and now we also had the Navy SeaBees to help.

The next few days were a whirlwind. The first day we put up two tents with the Alaska technicians and the SeaBees working with the Djibouti Army. I would be remiss if I didn't mention the friends I made who served in the Djibouti Army. Besides my friend Colonel Mohamad Farah and his fellow Colonel Fouad Elmi, who was in charge of transportation, I got to know many of the soldiers who assembled these tents. Colonel Elmi was a great help, and we could always count on him for transport, and he found the soldiers that were the ones who installed the tents. They were hardworking men, and I enjoyed working and spending time with them. The next day we built a tent for the Djibouti Army as a clinic for the many migrants sheltering from Somalia, Yemen, and Ethiopia. I was sad that we had booked our tickets to return before we finished. I missed the initial reason we had come to assemble three tents in that village above Lake Assal. I was glad to see the photos of the tents being used as schools knowing they were strong enough to last the constant winds blowing on that plateau, and see the children play with some of those soccer balls I have brought.

In Djibouti, I have found a country poised at the crossroads of many conflicts. Its neighbors Somalia, Yemen, and Ethiopia countries are often in turmoil. The Chinese have invested heavily in Africa, and you can see it in this country. One major project they were finishing was building a railroad from Ethiopia to the port in Djibouti. This will revolutionize opening up the resources from landlocked Ethiopia. The roads were often clogged with trucks, and now they could move cargo by rail. The Chinese have taken over a part of the port too, and have built an army base also. The Chinese come to a country building these projects importing their own workers and keeping them away from the population. My only fear is that one day the Chinese will want payment in full for their loans, and Djibouti will suffer for it. The Chinese give nothing for free so, when the loans come due and cannot be paid, they take over valuable parts of the country. I have hope that we will not forget to show the Djibouti people our support in the future.

If the work I have been doing in Nepal and Djibouti piques your interest to learn more, go to www.globalactioncoalition. org We are a 501c3 organization that has been working in Nepal and Djibouti, Africa, since 2009, helping women and children. Besides our ongoing projects working in the schools in Chitwan, Nepal, we are focusing on two other newer projects. Small-Dollar Loan Initiative for Women and Families in Nepal and Djibouti and an Online School and Library for Rural, Underserved Women in Southeast Europe. I can promise you 100% of your donations will contribute directly to programs.

photo: *Douda school tent*

chapter 19

GOLF AS A DEFINING MOMENT AND OTHER RUMINATIONS

I wanted to take a moment in this book to share some philosophy. I have a few tidbits garnered from various teachings that have worked, and perhaps someone reading this book will find them helpful.

I find Golf a game full of Defining Moments. Every shot has its challenges, and Golf is so personal. You may be playing with others, but you carry your own mental and emotional thoughts into each round. Some play Golf fearlessly, at least at some points. Most golfers will play the same courses and will have a history in your memory of your past efforts imprinted in your mind. As you prepare to tee off, you might remember that you hooked it in the trees last time you played. Or on the next hole, maybe you tried to cross the small water hazard in front but left that ball among many resting on the bottom. On the other hand, you may also have hit it across effortlessly.

We know how powerful our memories affect our body's performance. I hope you see the analogy. How can we leave our minor or significant failures behind and bring a beginner's mind into this shot? One of the unwritten rules of Golf is to not focus on your score. When I played the Babe, I remember a city course in Tampa named after famed woman golfer Babe Zaharias. Every hole seemed easy. I knew I was playing in the zone. A typical day in Golf, some parts of your game work, and others not. Right from the first driving off the tee, everything shot is right down the middle, but that chip shot at the green is too short or long. Or maybe your putting is speaking a foreign language today. This day on the 1st nine holes, they were all in agreement. Intuitively I knew that I should not count up my score at the turn before the second 9. The siren call was too much, and when I added up my score, I had shot a 36, a personal best. I think you can guess what happened on the stretch. I didn't fall apart, but the magic had dissipated. Some of the clubs decided to speak French and some Russian on some holes. I ended the round with a 46. An 82 was still the best round of golf I had ever played. I also knew if I had not thought about the score, I could have done better. In Golf, it is yourself that is the enemy or the best friend. You are not playing against anybody else. When you approach having to cross a water hazard or over the sand to get to the green, you must not see it. If it is not there in your mind, you hit the easy chip or drive, which is no big deal.

On the other hand, if you see it, it can be a magnet to your ball, and your body chokes up, and that easy swing loses its beauty and clunk and splash and say goodbye to that Titleist or Top Flight as it joins others waiting peacefully in its depths. Life is the same. You meet a person and start a relationship. Can you be present and enjoy the excitement, or will you start remembering the past failures and subconsciously sabotage the opportunity for love. Did that last person you were with hurt you in some way?

Will, you choke up in the shot and clunk it in the water for no reason other than the last time you faced this hole the ball dropped in.? You must find that Beginner's mind, and not see the water or remember the past failures in life. It is not only in playing sports or finding love that we sabotage ourselves. In this book, my friends I have brought to you have found themselves facing more than just a water hazard. Something happened to let them rise out of the past. They found the strength and the wisdom not to see only their fears or anger, which allowed their swing to be a thing of beauty. Once you begin that journey, it gets easier. That is why golfers keep on playing. Every golfer has that lousy round. Yet, the successes bring us back. You might have only a few good shots or putts at the beginning of playing the golf game. These are the secrets of knowing that you can do it. It is the same in life, and you can play the game, and you can learn to succeed.

In a funny corollary to the Golf Chapter I was on the tennis court the other day and two of my fellow players were struggling with their game. One kept hitting it long and was visibly upset. So I told him to adjust the screw on his racket. He actually looked at the racket for the screw. I said the actual screw is in your mind, but take out your virtual screwdriver and adjust the one you imagine is on the racket and see what happens. He started hitting his shot more accurately. The other player was just not feeling grounded and kept double faulting and missing easy shots. I told him that when that happens to me I go back to my Aikido training. I set me self in to a stance and work to feel the connection between my feet and the earth. It really has helped me. Another trick because it is tricking the mind to let go. Remember Yogi Berra said baseball was 50% physical and the other 90% was mental! I started doing this in my days playing racquet ball, when I was not feeling my game I would call for a substitution. My partner would look at me and then I would change my body posture and act like I was another player who was stepping in. They got a kick out of it, but for me it was a way to change my mindset which often changed the tenure of the game. Life is often changing our stance our mindset our preconceived notions and finally meeting the challenges we did not plan for.

Did Juan Ortiz not keep finding challenges in his learning to maneuver in his life in a wheelchair, and yet something pulled him forward to an extraordinary life. Azim, overwhelmed with grief, has turned that nightmare into a way of immortalizing his son and saving thousands of children from recreating more horrors. So I invite you to look at your own lives, forget your bad shots, forgive yourself, and begin to play the game of life fearlessly and with a beginner's mind. When I was getting a divorce, I was full of doubts about choosing to search for love and I had three holes in one in six months. Was that a sign or just my letting go of my doubting mind?

My other life's teachings that have worked and worked for me are another one I learned from the famous self-help guru, Wayne Dyer. He said we should be a partner with God in creating our own lives. He said it was as easy as three words.

INTENTION: Picture what you want in life. Is it true love, a better job, an opportunity to help shape the world? So right it down, using your imagination to see it and feel it. Got it?

ATTENTION: Now that you have something you want, you have to work towards it. Is it the love of your life? Well, maybe join Match or some other dating site. Is it a different job, well rewrite your resume and start your search. The interesting part is that it might not be that action will be the one responsible for making the connection, but perhaps better explained, it is the energy you have put forth that moves the universe into alignment. Now that you have pictured your dream and you have started working for it. Now let go. You have set the universe in motion, and you can relax. Still follow through with all that you have started, but the next part is, for me, the hardest but the most necessary

NO TENSION: It is said in Buddhist teachings, 'Attachment to outcome leads to suffering.' It does not mean it is not ok to want something; it is just not wanting it so bad you get in your own way. This time you will say to yourself. I know what I want, I have started working towards it, and now I will let it happen without worrying about it. I challenge you to try this and see if it works for you as it has worked for me. So now I will tell you one of my stories that illustrates this. Remember I say one, so you will have to trust me that there are more. I am still living in St. Petersburg, and I have a buyer for my gallery building in Tampa. Suzanne and I have started thinking it is time for us to buy a house and stop renting. We are walking our dogs around Bay Isle Drive, and Suzanne asks the question. What do you want in a house?. Without much thought, I said three things. 1. Privacy, as the house we lived in was close to others, as were the previous ones. 2. A place for a hot tub. All my houses in Tampa had a hot tub, and you could just open the lid and fall in. So soothing even in the summer. 3. Amazing! This came from the fact our first house, or rather condo, was in downtown St. Petersburg. It was a penthouse unit, and when you walked in, your first views were of the bay. It was magical. We could walk from our home to all the restaurants and coffee shops and along the waterside. It will always be a special place, and you can understand why I wanted amazing again. So fast forward a bit. I have sold my building, and my mother, who we had moved up to Largo from Boca Raton to be near us, passes away. She had always said she wanted to leave on her own terms while still getting around, and she did just that. In life's scheme of things, her timing was impeccable, and though I miss her dearly and the thing about calling her often, her passing allowed Suzanne to suggest we could now think about living where there are seasons.

So Suzanne remembering my fondness for Greenville, South Carolina starts searching that area. We decide to plan a July trip after the closing of the building to visit. Memorial Day is coming up, and Suzanne says she has found a house on Zillow that I need to see. The house on a golf course catches my eye too. She flies up quickly as our realtor friend, Mike Mumma, tells us that real estate moves fast. He is so right, and I am glad we listened. We put in an accepted offer, and our trip in July ends up beginning with the closing on the house and the beginning of a new life in an exceptional area. So the house, it off the street, and the neighbors on both sides are respectfully distant, and the golf course also is not right in the backyard, and with the 60 plus trees, we have quite a bit of privacy most of the year. Did I tell you about the hot tub that came with the house? Yep precisely right on the downstairs deck. The two upstairs decks are in the trees, so we call it the Tree House, and when you walk in the central area looking through the trees, you immediately think AMAZING! Maybe I had not considered where the house was, but I did get everything I asked for and more. So prepare your life for an adventure. Create the world you want and pay attention to those Defining Moments that you cross.

Epilogue

We come to the end of this book and of learning about these fantastic people. You will notice I finished with stories about my own exploits. I add myself with trepidation as these people I have chosen have incredible stories, and I, like yourself, find myself in awe of them. Yet, I have had many 'defining moments' that I have shared. The community work led me to meet and work with General Chip Diehl and introduce me to the Coalition to have Colonel Bharat Gurung and Colonel Samuel Alito over for a Thanksgiving dinner. Or having my daughter meet Elio Navarro and from that change in their lives to them inviting me to the disability world, or a chance meeting with Maestro Thomas Wilkins to me writing this book. These connections became opening doors to another world. These are some of my moments, how about you? Can you go back through your life and think of the defining moments that shaped you or the defining people who influenced you. Can you also remember the moments you did not take that other path? What I wish to leave you with is that we are on a trail that has many forks. Do not judge the choices as good or bad, but be aware as you get these opportunities; the question is, how will you face them? How will you support them if they take the more challenging road? I hope you will find excitement and joy on your journey and celebrate, and I thank you for entering this book; I hope you found some of these people's work inspiring; you will help them continue it and make the world a better place. Rob